CISTERCIAN STUDIES SERIES: NUMBER NINETEEN

CONTEMPLATIVE LIFE

CISTERCIAN STUDIES SERIES: NUMBER NINETEEN

CONTEMPLATIVE LIFE

Jean Leclercq OSB

translated by
Elizabeth Funder OSB

CISTERCIAN PUBLICATIONS
Kalamazoo, Michigan
1978

Cistercian Studies Series   ISBN 0-87907-800-6
This volume   ISBN 0-87907-819-7

Originally published by Éditions P. Lethielleux, Paris, as
Vie religieuse et vie contemplative.

Ecclesiastical permission to publish this book has been obtained from
Bernard Flanagan, Bishop of Worcester, September 28, 1972.

Available in Europe and the Commonwealth
from A.R. Mowbray & Co. Ltd.,
St Thomas House, Becket Street, Oxford OX1 1SJ.

CONTENTS

ABBREVIATIONS

CC   Corpus Christianorum, Series Latina (Turnhout: Brepols, 1945-).

CF   Cistercian Fathers Series (Spencer, Mass.-Washington, DC: Cistercian Publications, 1970-).

CS   Cistercian Studies Series (Spencer, Mass.-Washington, DC: Cistercian Publications, 1969-).

CSEL   Corpus Scriptorum Ecclesiasticorum Latinorum (Vienna: Hoelder-Pilcher-Tempsky).

RB   *Sancti Benedicti Regula Monasteriorum.* Ed. E. Manning (Westmalle: Typis Ordinis Cisterciensis, 1962).

SC   Sources Chrétiennes (Paris: Cerf, 1943-).

PREFACE

ONCE A MAN IS ON IN YEARS, he faces the publication of his quasi-posthumous works. This volume represents such a collection of articles and conferences.[1] They are not the work of my youth but of rather recent times. Although gathered together, they are yet quite disparate. Any thread of unity they show comes primarily from the fact that they were prompted by actual events—meetings and post-conciliar problems—and from the additional fact that most of them relate to a particular type of religious life, contemplative monasticism.[2] Thus the area under discussion is limited.

For the sake of order, it was necessary to group the various articles under a few headings and turn them into chapters. This arrangement takes for granted a general recognition of the relationship existing between religious life and contemplative life. Actually, contemplative life includes elements that are common to all other expressions of religious life; and these in turn, must also be characterized by what the Council

1. In each case where the article has been previously published, the place of publication is indicated in an initial note. Some of the chapters were reports to meetings and commisions and have not been previously published.

2. This has been true of three collections of articles published by Cerf and another appearing in this Series, *Aspects of Monasticism: Yesterday and Today* (CS 7). Several of the articles in *La liturgie et les paradoxes chrétiens* treat of contemplative prayer. The *Recueil d'études sur S. Bernard* (3 vols.) concern more the problems of literary criticism, although the third volume has a long study on St Bernard and the history of obedience.

[Vatican II] has termed "contemplation."[3] Two factors emerge then, namely, that the general renewal of religious life involves and directs a renewal of contemplative life; and secondly, that contemplative life stands as a reminder, helping all religious to clearer perception of some of the values which they must preserve.

In this period of crisis and confrontation, religious life itself is not being called into question—at least not within the Church. It does exist. But it must be adapted. It is evolving, but it must not be substantially changed. It remains essentially what it was, and it must continue to be that. Yet it is being reformed, in the sense of being led to adopt forms that are new by comparison with those it had assumed in the past. Hence the importance of distinguishing its permanent values from their changing expressions. This part of renewal, this need of rejuvenation must be kept well in mind from the outset. So, too, must the contribution which the young are making.

Relating the contemplative life to the broad context of renewal, we find the triple approach of solitude, prayer and penance appropriate. Tradition and Council both teach that these three basic elements, subject to definite interpretations that establish their meaning, distinguish this type of religious life from others.[4] Various problems will be dealt with—general and particular, doctrinal and practical; and our sifting of these will involve us in history, contemporary, as well as that of the near and distant past. The past is not to be confused with tradition—which is transmission to the present—though it certainly sheds light on the present. It not only prepares the material, so to speak, but shows us what was profitable and what was not, what was conditioned by passing circumstances and what, by contrast, was permanent. This, in turn, gives us clear convictions as to what is to be retained now, and what rejected.

The future of the contemplative life in the "young churches" (as the Council calls them), a future just beginning, will test

3. *Perfectae caritatis,* 5.

4. *Perfectae caritatis,* 7. The appropriate statements of the Council are cited in the course of this volume.

the vitality of the contemplative life. Moreover, the lessons emerging from the fairly recent implantation of monasticism in Africa and Asia will show us that, even though there are problems and difficulties, there is no lack of imagination or courage in the quest for their solution. The Spirit of God will come to help our incapacity, disclosing new forms while sacrificing none of the essential and truly traditional values.

There was once someone who knew well how to unite in her person and even in her motherhood the entire heritage of the Jewish people and the full life of the Church which came to birth in her. Mary, the Mother of Jesus Christ, is the model for the blending of promise and fulfillment. She both received and gave us the One who has renewed all things by entering into our human history. And, as someone has written—"Christ is the answer to all problems."

CHAPTER I

TRADITION AND EVOLUTION IN RELIGIOUS LIFE[1]

THERE ARE SEVERAL WAYS of developing this topic. We might, for example, give a statement of principles—but this method involves the risk of bogging down in the abstract and producing only generalities. Or we could examine a few points that call for renewal and show how to effect it—but this method might involve us in details only, and leave no hope of covering them all. A middle course will be adopted here. We shall first make a general survey of our problems, describing some of the attempts at their solution on various levels. Then we shall illustrate our conclusions with a few examples.

QUESTIONS POSED BY HISTORY

When we speak of "renewing" religious life, we mean the same as renewing anything else. The word itself shows clearly enough that there is no question of starting from scratch, but rather of revitalizing a reality that could well be wearing out through age. Our task is to rejuvenate. In this process some elements will disappear or recede, others will be restored or improved, and others still that have long been overlooked, will show up in the foreground. The real problem is one of continuity in evolution—a continuity that has been maintained in the past and is still to be sought in our present phase. But before we can sift the changing from the permanent, we need to distinguish the principles that justify evolution, indicating its limits as well as its significance.

1. *Revue diocésaine de Tournai* 22 (1967): 398-420.

1

If you want an answer, you must first state your problem. Now, we are faced with a possible transformation of religious life, for both past and present show that things have changed and are changing. To assess the past, we would need to paint a huge historical fresco, showing the different trends as they succeeded each other or converged. Then we should have to work out what factors have remained constant.[2] The difficulty of sketching such a tableau arises from the many contingent factors that seem to crop up all at once—factors that have elements in common certainly, but also deep-rooted differences. And the most important of them have a personal character. It is not a matter of examining the development of institutions, even supposing they existed from the beginning, rather it is a question of examining charismatic phenomena within the Church—for her institutions are brought to birth, then modified, diversified and multiplied by such charisms.

From the Church's earliest times, some Christians were called to consecrate themselves to God in a special way. When these Christians were drawn to live together, they formed the nucleus of associations, groups and categories, though they did not constitute a pre-existing "state of life"—a *status* in the sense that Roman law gives to the word—but rather, corresponded to what the older terminology called *ordo, taxis, tagma*—that is, groups of the faithful more or less organized and following a rather similar vocation. At the beginning, the exclusive purpose was to sanctify oneself in order to be saved. One might perhaps perform some works of service for others, but these works were not sought as an end in themselves. They were not an inherent part of religious life in its original form.

From early antiquity right through to the present, we have the members of the Church falling into three classes, corresponding to the description given in the preface for one of the prayers in the Good Friday liturgy: "Let us pray for all

2. In two articles entitled "Points de vue sur l'histoire de l'état religieux" in *La vie spirituelle* 74 (1946): 816-833; 75 (1946): 127-137, I tried to write this sketch. Since then, with the aid of recent research, the project has been realized by F. Petit: "La vie religieuse—Son histoire" in *Au seuil de la théologie* (Paris, 1966), 3:321-355.

bishops, priests, deacons, subdeacons, acolytes, exorcists, lectors, porters (i.e., the clerics), confessors, virgins, widows (i.e., the ascetics), and all the people of God (i.e., the simple laity)."

This threefold division setting the faithful who lead an ascetic life apart from the simple laity, is present throughout the whole course of tradition.[3] It is not an indication of the relative worth of Christians in these different categories, or of their virtue or holiness, great or small, but rather, of the difference between their functions in the Church and the conditions in which they lead the Christian life.

This gives us two special categories among the faithful, the hierarchical and the ascetical. The first applies to those in priestly orders: bishops, priests and clerics, including subdeacons and those in minor orders. These constitute the clergy: their role is to live in service of the altar and to minister to men. The second category is a purely spiritual one; for some of the faithful, here referred to as "confessors, virgins and widows," order their whole lives to the practice of Christian virtue for the sake of personal sanctification. Others live an ordinary life in the world, though they endeavor, more or less, to sanctify it by fidelity to the practice and spirit of religion. This last category constitutes the mass of the Christian people, described by the early Fathers and by the liturgy as a "holy people,"[4] for they have received the Holy Spirit who is given to the entire community of the Church.

Parallel to the hierarchy, then, there existed from very early times a class of people whom Duchesne describes as an "aristocracy" in the community of the faithful. They had various names—ascetics, celibates, encratics, religious, confessors. Women were represented by consecrated virgins and by widows, those who embraced continency in their widowhood after only a short period of married life. These lived in their own homes; and their state has been described as "domestic

---

3. A few instances are quoted in P. de Puniet, *The Roman Pontifical* (Paris, 1931) 2:64.

4. E.g. in the Canon of the Mass: *Plebs tua sancta*; in the Secret of the Mass, *Cognovi* (Common of Virgins): *Sanctae plebis oblatio*. The Fathers in their sermons often addressed themselves to the faithful in the words: "Your holiness."

monasticism." They really constituted secular institutes, but it was a long time before they were called this and a long time, too, before they became the concern of bishops and councils. As an institution they are often overlooked by historians, although they lasted right through the mediaeval period.

In the third century the new phenomenon of monasticism appeared. It developed along two main lines, symbolized by the names of St Antony and St Augustine. St Antony, "the father of monks," is the best known of those solitaries who retired into the desert.

At the beginning, these lived apart from the world, in isolation. Later they lived in groups. They are hermits, and their type of life will always exist. But the anchoretical life, though fervent, was not sufficiently organized, and gave rise to extremes that are often sublime but sometimes open the door to abuses. There were those who deprived themselves of sleep or lodging, others who ate only herbs, those who went about almost without clothing, others who wore chains and fetters, those who went looking for rebuffs, others who remained standing and immobile, those who lived in ditches or pits—and other types still more bizarre. Some were saints and were followed by imitators. But there was a constant effort to organize the monastic life and to avoid the deviations it might engender. These abuses would be remedied by cenobitism, which is life in common, under a rule and an abbot. This new phase in evolution developed under men of God like St Pachomius and St Basil in the East, and St Benedict in the West. Each legislated in his own way, but commonly they all appeal to Sacred Scripture, and especially to the Gospels, as the source of a monk's obligations. Later, their disciples and successors would take up charitable, cultural or apostolic works according to the exigencies of time and place. But these works never became the goal, even the secondary goal, of the monastic institution.

In the West, moreover, bishops like St Augustine were responsible for the development of a clerical form of monasticism. Historians on the whole have not attributed to this form the importance it warrants. From the eighth century, the life of the clerks regular was called canonical, and from the eleventh it experienced a great revival. It involves activity—that of the pastoral charge, the care of souls—as one of its ends. These two institutions of regular life, monastic and canonical, are quite distinct and separate, though each has influenced the other.

In the West, from the twelfth century onwards, new religious orders arose to meet the new needs of the Church. Here again, contingent circumstances condition the response and direct it. The Crusades called forth the military orders dedicated to warfare for the reconquest of the Holy Places or the defence of oppressed Christians. The hospitaller orders cared for the poor and the sick in the Holy Land and elsewhere. There were others devoted to the ransom of captives, their members freely accepting captivity as a condition for the ransom of others, thus risking privation of the support and security of religious life for long periods while in the hands of infidels. In the thirteenth century different circumstances and aspirations gave rise to the Friars Preacher and Friars Minor.

Gradually over the following centuries certain ascetics, both clerical and lay, who were not and did not want to be monks, organized some Christians into communities which they felt called to found. All these institutions have had great charismatic souls at their origin—men like St Francis of Assisi and St Dominic. Generally speaking, their members had no intention of withdrawing into solitude, but rather of giving their activity to the service of the Church. As new needs arose, new forms of apostolic or charitable work arose to meet them; some institutes, like the Society of Jesus, employed their members in different types of work—teaching, retreats, preaching, missions; others specialized in a particular activity, like teaching, or devotion to the poor and the sick, or any form of human need.

In summarizing this long evolution, we must be wary of reducing it to an artificial order. In this field as in all others, life was complex. Once you try to over-organize the facts, you risk not seeing how they really developed, and what they mean in sum total—for there was a good deal of interaction.

All this led to variety, change, mutual influence, blending. But at least we can distinguish two principal phases. The first, as we saw, witnesses to the search for God alone. The call was a call to salvation—not to a particular or superior type of sanctity. "What am I to do if I am going to be saved?" was the question the newcomer in the desert asked his spiritual father. St Benedict presents entrance to the monastery as the means by which one who was called worked out his salvation. He did not come to the monastery to become a saint, to become holier than others or because he was already holy. And he did not stay in the monastery because he had become a saint— but because he was not one, and he knew it. His call was to give all—and to give it in love. This kind of aspiration can only be a gift of the Holy Spirit. Thus we have a class of Christian men and women wanting nothing else but God, following their personal vocations, seeking fulfillment together. St Benedict does not call upon altruistic motives when he speaks of entrance into the monastic life. Other means and other ends need not be excluded, but they are not an integral part of the religious vocation, or at least, not of all religious vocations. Moreover, no insistence on a "specific service" or a "particular function"—even in the order of witness or prayer—can explain the nature of vocations to the monastic life in past centuries nor in certain cases at the present time in the West—and never in the East. The call to work out one's salvation in a particularly difficult way is a true charism. And the early Church acknowledged this by considering it her duty to pray for her ascetics every bit as much as she counted on their prayer for her.

In the second phase of the history of the religious life, something is added to this basic theme of the search for God. We now find the additional desire to perform some service for the Church, so that by fulfilling this task one could be saved and sanctified. It even developed that this secondary goal became the primary one: one chose to carry out some apostolate or charity in the religious life, regarding the latter as a means for helping the work.

This brief survey of the past shows the importance of the area in which changes have occurred: it involves the relationship between dedication of oneself to God and activity taken on in the service of the Church. At present, this relationship between consecration to God and the goal of the apostolate or charity is constituting a problem for some, especially where the secondary goal can be achieved, and sometimes better achieved—in better conditions and with better results—apart from the religious life. It is a serious problem. History indicates its origins and even suggests a solution. There has been a reversal of values over the centuries. Should we now revert to the original order? One cannot insist that every vocation to a consecrated life should add a secondary purpose which is to be taken as part and parcel of the religious state—for it long existed, and still exists in some institutes, with no secondary aim to all. On the other hand, there is a priority to be preserved or recovered, a harmony to be established or re-established, between dedication to God and the practical works which may derive from this. Again, we need to distinguish between the vocation, which is a charism, and the institution, within which it reaches its fulfillment. It may be that the balancing of this relationship does not need too much logical exposition—the Gospel tells us that we consecrate ourselves to God only to contribute to the coming of the kingdom, both in ourselves and in others. In the course of time, one or other aspect has been stressed according to the changing environment created by the grouping of vocations.

In the past, these changes were responses to changing circumstances or aspirations. And in the present, things are changing still. Our era witnesses new developments both in the world and in the Church. These developments are bound to have repercussions in the religious life. What are they, then? Can they be foreseen or anticipated? Can they be controlled—or must we submit to them with regret? We might be tempted to deny that there are any problems—or to consider them unimportant. We might concede that so long as the essential and interior elements remain, then the exterior and accessory may be modified—the religious habit, for example, or the form of enclosure for nuns—grilles, curtains, turns and the network of locks and bolts. But this is an over-simplification. The fact that many externals can and must change is really secondary. Is the inner heart of the religious institution to have no growth? The total gift of self to God always remains the central point. But between this essential inner attitude and the externals, between the basic consecration and the exterior forms of its development, there is real relationship. The changes effected in man, in the world and in the Church can lead to a modification of perspective, a deeper habit of reflection and a renewal of understanding for the interpretation of the traditional heritage, giving greater flexibility to its institutions. All this is fraught with risks—and the possibility of deviation is never absent. So before we sift the realities that do not change and those that do, we need to establish some principles as a guide for clear discernment.

EVOLUTION AND TRADITION

Tradition is a fair guide in estimating the legitimacy and limits of any development, for it implies openness to the present. This is as true of religious life as of other realities. No need here to elaborate the idea or to explain it further[5]— we will simply reduce it to Heidegger's definition: "Tradition does not hand us over to the restrictions of a past that is over and done with: *Ueberliefern*, to deliver, signifies a liberation leading to the freedom of dialogue with what was."[6] Tradition results from experience accumulated for generations, but it is not their sum total added up once and for all allowing for no further additions. It preserves the heritage it has received, but only to foster new spiritual development; it must be ever reliving that heritage. It is no mere string of customs that are to be reproduced and passed on intact. What are sometimes referred to, in some houses, as "the traditions" or "our traditions" are no more than customs or practices. Perhaps they do no more than standardize past experiences. When this happens development is baulked in the cause of

5. In *Chances de la spiritualité occidentale* (Paris, 1966), pp. 67-85, I tried to do this in the articles "Tradition et ouverture."
6. *Qu'est-ce que la philosophie?* (Paris, 1957), p. 17.

handing on customs unaltered. On the contrary, tradition, understood as the flow of life in both nature and grace, is a continuous experience, ever in process. It absorbs new values and eliminates peripheral elements. But this twofold operation is not automatic; it requires man's courage and intelligence. He needs discretion when lopping off dead branches to give the sap free flow.

As there is tradition and traditions, or if you like, Tradition and tradition, so too there is Evolution and evolution. At the heart of any great evolution transmitting the essential and permanent elements by living them, there is room at the same time for smaller evolutions, maintaining or modifying, to some extent, the merely accessory. These two elements are clearly connected and yet different; our task is to relate them and to give each its point of departure. They could be considered as two different dimensions of the same mystery of man in the Church.

The first derives primarily from human nature itself, which remains basically unchanged and from the mystery of Christ in his first coming, when he assumed this nature and lived in it, using it to inaugurate a Church that was to last forever. This Church was endowed with life and grace for her growth and development. We acquire once and for all whatever is part of this first dimension. But there is a second, involving the world as it exists in each succeeding age—for us this is the world of the right now, ever on the move toward fulfillment, ever alert for the return of Christ. And, in addition, for religious there is the charism of their founder which in some way is related to a particular moment of time.

The tradition of the religious life will always find its source in the mystery of Christ and in the charism of each founder. Its real Evolution in the direction of eternal life begins there. But because of our insertion in time, this Tradition and Evolution take on particular and limited forms, giving rise to traditions and evolutions. Among these necessary expressions, some seem to hold a privileged place being carried over to every new foundation and surviving every period of renewal. These are the elements which must be recognized and fostered as particularly apt for the transmission of the Tradition and the promotion of the Evolution. Real Evolution is always a return to authentic Tradition.

In religious life, Tradition is twofold, for it is related both to Christ and to the particular founder. This duality is a source of tension. The mystery of Christ is ever the same, but it is extended by a charism granted in the sixth century, or the sixteenth, or any other, and is therefore expressed in the psychological, cultural and institutional forms of that particular period. It is certainly to our own gain when the grace of our vocation clearly matches a charism received in earlier times by a man of God; there we find an incentive, a guide and a guarantee. But it also begets a difficulty that must not be disguised but faced squarely if we are going to overcome it. Religious orders are not dispensed from sifting and groping, in their effort to foster a homogeneous evolution—for the founder's charism will not appear identical to all on the same day or with the same clarity!

The role of Tradition and Evolution, then, is to instill in the heart of our life the whole mystery of Christ: the redemptive Incarnation, the paschal mystery and the final victory of good over evil begun here and now in the Church. Our sinful nature tends to dull and obscure this insight, because it has to express itself in forms that are subject to all the deficiencies of the merely human. We are indeed blessed that the Holy Spirit comes to help our weakness: in every era and every institute he helps men to express the mystery of Christ and in the societies which they constitute, thus manifesting Tradition in traditions and expresses Evolution through evolutions. Thus does the Spirit lead us to new traditions and make possible a new and homogeneous evolution. True tradition, then, ensures the clear witness of grace and manifests in some way the paschal mystery. Legitimate evolution restores this transparency of grace to forms still capable of holding it, eliminating the rest. On the other hand, traditions or evolutions are dangerous once they tend to become opaque, to stand as absolute and definitive values in this world or to set up any goal to which the life of the Spirit in persons and in institutes must be subordinate.

Between these two extremes, there is a full gamut of possibilities, for different traditions and evolutions can co-exist. A man cannot change without preserving continuity with the past—nor can an institution: evolution always arises from traditional elements. Between these two poles, discernment can be operative only under the light of the Spirit and by our constantly striving for purity of heart. Growth in purity is the Church's abiding need, and what applies to the whole is true of each of her members, personally and in their various groups. The various institutions of the religious life, and in fact the life itself, all experience this need. Each of those who live this life is called to continual conversion—not only for his personal salvation and sanctification, but because he is responsible for the whole body of which he is part. From this point of view, new foundations are to be encouraged, as being so many forms of continuous renewal; but one day, not far off, these too will stand in need of self-reform. The Orders of Fontevrault and Grandmont have disappeared, and many others along with them. The same will certainly happen to some orders existing today. God decides these things; but there have been times when men have not made the necessary effort at renewal, or when these efforts have not been made in the right direction. History shows that delays can be final and irremediable— sound warning, indeed, of the importance and yet the greatness of the times we live in, and the possibilities of the future.

THE PERMANENT AND THE CHANGEABLE

Once the general principles of an evolution deep in the heart of a tradition have been recalled, it is possible to indicate some areas of application posed by present day problems. To form sound judgments, we need to relate to the past and to consider the present just as God allows it to be.

There would seem to be no need to insist here on what remains unchanged: Vatican II has done so authoritatively in Chapter Six of *Lumen Gentium* and in the Decree *Perfectae Caritatis*. No one would think of questioning the fact that there does exist in the Church a religious life, irreducible to any of its elements, but made up of the ensemble of them.

Some of these will be, or have already been modified, but the central fact sustaining and unifying all—that is, the special consecration and total gift of self to God—has no orders to disappear. History shows that the past had many vicissitudes, and it prepares us for more in the future—but the charisms of the Spirit stand firm, as transmitted to us in the great experiences of the founders and reformers, from St Anthony to Charles de Foucauld and our own day. All are part of the progressive fulfillment of the eschatological kingdom. The shadow of this passing world has to some extent renewed, moulded or influenced these forms in the course of time. But here we make no claim at all to be assessing all the aspects of this paradox. We will simply give one rather important example —that of obedience—and add a few other points of special interest.

We may as well give up all hope of saying anything original about obedience, after all that has been written about it in the last few years, but two points are clear: the mystery of our participation in the redemptive obedience of Christ must not be lost sight of but rather brought into fuller light by the New Testament teaching and Church tradition; and on the other hand, in the past and even now, some of the forms assumed in practice by the exercise of authority and obedience in the Church have been influenced by elements deriving not from the Gospel but from a combination of the social and psychological context of certain periods. Paul VI described this perfectly at a general audience on July 25, 1965: "Experience and history show us samples of authority, especially ecclesiastical authority, that are neither faithful nor felicitous. The whole notion of authority in the Church must be deepened and purified of unessential elements." We need the help of exegesis, history and theology in this work of clarification.

But evangelical obedience was not deformed through the factors influencing its theory and practice in the past—factors which were themselves inevitable. Our present civilization could well enrich the form in which obedience is expressed today. New ideas and aspirations are springing up in the Western world that are strangely in accord with aspirations drawn from the

Gospel and promoted by the Decree *Perfectae Caritatis.* These new ideas are no substitute, nor are they sufficient on their own, but they can give form to Gospel aspirations and show us how they will be fulfilled.

Think over, for a minute, the problem of "structures." There was a time when any society or enterprise would have a head at the top (no matter what he was called—chief, patron, director, superior) and then under him a staff, subordinates, subjects—in a word, "inferiors." Today this hierarchy has to make room for a new class of collaborators—the technical and specialized advisors whom the head really needs, and without whom he cannot fulfill his role. This is certainly a phenomenon in civilization. A General Confederation of experts for an entire group of industries has a review called *Présence-Energie* describing this new phenomenon as follows: "Directors have to face increasingly difficult situations involving considerable means and information, and also demanding exceptionally prompt reaction and often prompt decision; it is important that no mistake be made. Any error on their part may have consequences that are lightning-quick and often fatal for the organism they are directing; consequences affecting, perhaps, a large number of people. As a result it has become almost impossible to cope unaided with situations and necessary decisions. And it is vital to ensure more time for reflection and to cultivate openness."

The writer of the article speaks of "the necessity of having experts who are responsible for thinking over certain broad, basic themes, or studying more general questions," and continues:

"The experiments we have conducted in this field prove that this type of co-operation is both possible and productive. It does not overturn the authority of the hierarchical structure (which sometimes seems to be over-cautious), or the authority and efficacy of the one in charge. Quite the contrary. But it demands that both head and members really adapt themselves to the evolution with courage and clarity. Once these conditions are fulfilled, we have seen for ourselves that authority is actually strengthened by its recognition of the actual problem as stated by the experts, and by its endeavor to effect the real decentralization thus expressed."[7]

Certainly, this can result in misunderstanding, and argument, but these show all the more clearly "the necessity for exchange, co-operation and dialogue, which are no mere norms but permanent values."

Religious orders have something to learn from these new patterns in the business world, which are proving their worth today. The practical role of both council and community in government might well be renewed and rejuvenated along these lines—for the mentality of recent times relegated to quite a secondary place this practice which monastic and religious Rules had introduced.

Everyone is aware that especially in the West new techniques and electronic computers, and even the progress of commerce are affecting our methods of information, pedagogy and teaching, as well as the forms of culture and social structures. For example, professors will now step down from their platforms. Until now, in periods of stability, the mature or elderly seniors or "ancients" were venerated as the witnesses to tradition; but in periods of evolution you do not find the same respect given them. Even the purpose of their professional activity is obscured. This will not prevent their finding another place in secular or religious society, but a definite change has taken place. In the same way, other peoples—in Africa, Asia, and elsewhere—can express obedience in forms belonging to their own civilization. There is no question of substitution here: we are not saying that our obedience as religious imitating Christ can now be replaced by the forms of submission to authority that are observable in every type of society toward those responsible for the common good. But religious obedience includes the secular and gives it a sanctifying value. Our task will be to reconcile the mystery of fraternal service as expressed in ministry within the Church, with all that is good in the

7. A. Gros and M. Aumont, "Réflexion sur l'évolution générale du problème des cadres" in *Présence-Energie,* no. 461: "Bulletin de la quinzaine de l'Union nationale des cadres de la maîtrise Eau-Gaz-Electricité" reproduced in a supplement to the *Bulletin of C.T.N.* (Centre d'étude des conséquences générales des grandes Techniques nouvelles) 6, no. 40 (January 1967).

psychology and organization of every era and every environment. Vast horizons lie open before us!

With these few practical considerations on the changeable and the unchangeable in the area of obedience (which we took by way of example), we can now deal more briefly with other problems.

The changeable element is the form for expressing the realization of certain secondary ends. Sometimes, perhaps, even these secondary ends themselves must be changed, when they no longer fulfill the purpose behind their historical origin. We have a clear example of this in those orders founded to ransom captives from the Saracens. Providing that the sense of proportion is preserved, the same criterion may be applied to other secondary ends. For example, in countries where every kind of evangelization is forbidden because of political and religious conditions, teaching no longer fulfills the same role as when it went hand in hand with evangelization. Again, the care of the sick, who would otherwise have no hope of receiving the witness of religion, presents a similar problem. It does not follow that such activities have no purpose now; but this purpose has undergone modifications that call it into question.[8]

Again, the changeable element in religious life is represented by new ways of approaching certain ancient and permanent realities. For example, in the sphere of poverty, we have both the current and the conciliar insistence on the need for witness or testimony, which should be collective. This is something new, or renewed, when compared with the ideas of other periods in the past—especially the recent past. And there are similar problems of the same kind regarding voluntary celibacy as a particular form of chastity. It is not so much the practice of chastity that has changed—any more than the vices opposed to it—but the psychological attitude and religious approach to both. History has seen periods of open, almost brutish license, followed by periods of exaggerated prudery, followed again by periods of excessive freedom. As with vice, so with virtue—attitude has varied according to the time. Today finds

8. Cf. "Esprit," *Vieillesse et vieillissement* 5 (May 1963): 904-910.

this subject receiving deeper consideration. Its full meaning is being studied in the light of the New Testament. A strong current of contemporary thought is laying greater stress on the fact that God has made man to live in relationship to himself and to others; and also on the fact that man fulfills himself in the giving that this relationship implies. Celibacy seems to deny one form of this relationship; but in fact, it is motivated by an attraction for the absolute relationship with God, and a relationship with others that will be purer and (in its immediate scope) less limited than in marriage. In a word, it is becoming increasingly clear that the first definition of man is that he is a being-in-relation, and from this point of view we must today reconsider him entirely.[9] This affects one's ideas on chastity within marriage—and also on celibacy. Both the acts and restrictions deriving from each of these states are now seen in a perspective of the whole which shows up the positive and the beautiful. The ethic has sometimes been no more than mere casuistry—but now, as with the early Fathers of the Church, new light has been thrown on it through reflection on the mystery of union and love: for this is the charity that requires detachment, that goes beyond its own interest—and therefore must effect the full development of the whole personality. The meaning of virginity has developed, and so too has the role of femininity in the whole existing order of things, including those who freely consecrate their celibacy to God. That spiritual liberty—which involves much more than being master of oneself—which is found in friendship is not a monopoly of canonized saints. The ideal it presents must be part of the formation given to each religious.[10]

As for the role of the liturgy in religious life, there has been considerable evolution, especially in the manner of participation, and everything points to the possibility of further changes here. In the early ages, consecrated virgins were placed in the front rows of the assembled congregation, where they could be seen—so striking was the example of their Christian witness.

9. Cf. M. Oraison, *Le mystère humain de la sexualité* (Paris, 1966).

10. Cf. R. Kanel and M. Delbrel, "La femme, le prêtre et Dieu" in *Supplément de la Vie spirituelle* 4 (1950): 151-161.

But from about the end of the middle ages they have been hidden away behind grilles and curtains. Religious (even non-cloistered) receive communion in a separate chapel, apart from the parish community—or any other. Will this continue? Analogous changes could easily be mentioned here, regarding the importance attributed in the religious life to the Eucharist and to the manner of its celebration. Again, the role of the priesthood, in both active communities and in contemplative communities not involved in the pastoral ministry, now constitutes a problem for many. There is reason for this.[11]

The psychological forms and exterior expression of some observances are changing. We borrow a few examples from the monastic life here—there are, of course, corresponding points in other forms of religious life. The question of enclosure has become so obvious that we do not need to stress it—and fortunately, the Christian aspiring to holiness is no longer reduced to the alternative *murus aut maritus*—enclosure or marriage.[12]

The religious habit provides another classic example—Pope Paul recently stated the essentials in regard to this matter.[13] The habit is an accessory element, and quite literally an external one—yet its evolution could well serve as a test case for the evolution of monasticism itself. St Benedict prescribes no particular color, provided that the material be not costly. In the eleventh century, however, black was insisted on, necessitating extra expense in weaving, dyeing and spinning. In the twelfth century there was a switch to grey in the new Orders, who wanted undyed cloth in its natural state, as a symbol of their return to simplicity and poverty. But very soon—and for these very same religious—white was required—and white the habit has remained, involving even more expense than black.

At present, several new foundations are returning to grey, quite spontaneously, and for the same reasons as in the twelfth

11. Cf. F. Petit, *loc. cit.,* p. 352; B. Webb, "Monastic aggiornamento" in *Downside Review* 85 (1967): 1-15.

12. Quoted in F. Petit, *loc. cit.,* p. 347.

13. Allocution to the Superiors General of Religious Congregations of Women, March 7, 1967. Text in *Documentation Catholique* 64 (1967), col. 584.

century.[14] The scapular was originally a working garment (*propter opera,* St Benedict said); then it became so long that it had to be taken off for work. Today it is one of the first victims of aggiornamento, and many a monk is glad to see it disappear, in the humorous realization that St Benedict himself regarded it as an extra—for work. The amount of material needed for some religious habits—like the full Benedictine cowl, with its wide sleeves—on top of the tunic and scapular, has caused some to think—and say—that mother could clothe her whole family with it. By returning to clothing similar to what is worn by the lay folk of ordinary means, would we not witness to both the poverty and simplicity of a state of life which should not draw notice to itself either by a resemblance to the clerical state or by a singularity devoid of significance. The habit may be a sign of consecration; but it may also separate us so much from other people that we feel no bond with them. Surely one can be a stranger to the world without being strange.

Another example of a custom retained merely because of antiquity is the manner in which most monks and nuns have their meals. They sit along the length of refectory walls, which must be proportionately long and expensive according to the number of people. The practice probably comes from the old Roman custom of eating without having neighbors across the table—and partly too from the monumental buildings of the middle ages. Our custom here involves a good deal of difference from that in the world. Just think of the space employed, the number of tables, their shape, placement and equipment, as well as the exigencies of serving them. All these demands are special, differing entirely from the way in which all classes of people everywhere in the world take their meals. These are not needs that can be justified as having any intrinsic connection with life consecrated to God. Is anyone going to insist that they are an aid to recollection? A poor type of recollection it must be! But perhaps there is some remote

14. Evolution is regressive if an Order today adopts white for all its members, including those who had kept grey or a colour approaching that.

resemblance to the solemn liturgy of the Eucharist? This would be ample justification, But, like the Eucharist, the meal is an essentially communitarian act. Why not sit facing each other, then? And if we press the point that for several reasons, two neighbors are better than four, we certainly make the meal something different from what it is meant to be—we make it an act of egoism in community.

The forms of fraternal correction give us another example of observance much changed through the centuries and in need of still more change. Early monasticism practised it privately, as the Gospel requires. Then it became the Chapter of Faults with public self-accusation and also reciprocal accusations without any preparation. The observance became more and more a rite, and so there was increasing difficulty in perceiving the Gospel counsel that lay at its origin.

Again, we have changes in asceticism, which must be adapted to the human equilibrium of modern man as it is found in the different civilizations; otherwise it does not foster an atmosphere of openness, and suffering becomes unhealthy. Today's needs in hygiene and sleep are not those of yesterday. There are many more of those whom the Germans call *Abend-typen*—"night owls." These find it difficult to adapt to so-called traditional horariums that call for the very early rising of the peasants and even the townsfolk of former days. You hear talk and discussion nowadays about the maladies of civilization which are new in Western society and not yet evident in any other. Problems of dietetics and asceticism are not the same in underfed countries as in those that have plenty. Forms of fatigue are not the same at different ages, not the same everywhere, not the same now as formerly.[15] The rhythm guiding both the development and utilization of the energies of young men and women religious, of superiors and of staff, is not the same and does not present the same problems. And among these problems we have to face that of vacations.

Finally, there is a change in the relationship between work time and leisure time—and we have to admit that this relationship changes from one generation to another, from one civi-

15. Cf. *CTN* 40 (January 1967): 3 and 10.

lization to another, and even within the same civilization. We are well aware of the possibilities of a future "era of leisure," and this era may be in the immediate future. It will suffice here to give one example from many available: "The scientific and technological development which brings leisure to workers is not the exclusive privilege of capitalists. The USSR is also concerned with this problem and is making efforts to improve her structures regulating the use of time not spent at work, so as to foster the physical and spiritual development of the person."[16]

In the meantime, many countries still need to work more. The members of those religious orders which are reputed as austere are sincerely asking themselves before God whether indeed they have an easier life than many of our contemporaries who are slaves to a work that is uncompromisingly regular, continuous, often monotonous and sometimes completely exhausting. The privilege of an austere life exempt from such hardship is only justifiable if balanced by a spiritual life that is absolutely self-emptying and intense. There may be no basic solution to such a problem, but it is good that it exists and is experienced. Progress depends not only on the modification of ideas and observances, but on the shouldering of full personal responsibility by every single monk and nun.

We need to let ourselves be hollowed out by grace, emptied of all egoism and wide open to love; and such a work of God in sinful man is not achieved without cost. The good conscience that comes from peace and spiritual liberty is bought only at this price.

CONCLUSION: THE GEARING OF INNOVATION

There can be no renewal without innovation. We must restore to full prominence those elements deriving from our origins—or from the Origin which is the Spirit of the Risen Christ. These original elements vitalize every period and re-

---

16. Extracts from *New Times* (Moscow 1966) and *Moscow News* (1966) quoted in *CTN* 40 (January 1967): 19.

main ever present—but they may have aspects which have grown old or have been forced into the background.

For renewal, then, we need to find fresh and (in this sense) new forms for the historical and provisional realizations of this permanent charism which transcends all time. The Council suggests this unhesitatingly in regard to poverty: "Let it be expressed in new forms"[17]—but it makes no attempt to prescribe them. They must come from the initiative of those who are docile to the Spirit and alert to the signs of the times. And in other fields, for example that of liturgy, the Council calls for innovation— "a new rite is to be made up."[18] Let us not fear this, or continue to sidestep the labor it involves. It is the easy way out to retain only what has always been in existence, or even to criticize old observances and superannuated ideas without making the effort to substitute new ones. A generation that can turn the work of Vatican II to profit by the power of the Holy Spirit, will prove equal to the task of incorporating the Council's ideas into its actual living.

A thirteenth-century writer said of his own epoch that: "The more youthful our age is, the more clearsighted it will be."[19] Why should not our own period merit the praise this Christian gives his? More so in fact, for it is not only modern but "new" with the powerful renewal effected by so many changes in the world and by Vatican II.

In the Church and in the religious life, we still need to cultivate this capacity for innovation—could we call it a virtue even?—for it will enable us to face fearlessly the future shock.

One of history's functions is to make us more imaginative—and as we witness the changeable elements in what we still have, history helps us to create in our minds a future as different from the present as the past was. It plays a role, then, in the education of the creative imagination which some consider so urgent today. A modern writer recently wrote: "in order to assimilate during one's lifetime those changes

17. *Perfectae caritatis*, 13.
18. *Sacrosanctum concilium*, 69, etc.
19. *Aetas nostra quo iunior, eo perspicacior.*—Rolandinus, *Summa*, quoted by G. Orlandelli in *Studi medievali* 6 (1965) II, 346.

that used to take centuries to evolve, modern man needs to provide himself with a broader idea of what is in store for him. The first task then is to try to shape this picture: he will need to accustom himself to reflect not only on today's short-term promises to the individual, but also on what the present holds for future generations. We teach our children the history of the past. Why not teach them to speculate on the future, to explore its possibilities and probabilities? We can learn to use our imagination about the ethical, psychological, political or social consequences of the technological advances, for their direction is clear. Moreover, we can train ourselves in the techniques of forecasting and learn how to use scientific methods in general. This does not mean that more courses in biology and physics are needed, but rather, more philosophical and logical reflection—with an institute exclusively devoted to the studies, the research and the provisional or prospective reports published by all the disciplines the world over."[20]

"I am afraid we have no imagination—we contemplatives at any rate", a nun said in her reply to a recently published enquiry.[21] This deficiency is not monopolized by contemplatives! There are all sorts of theories about the existing situation, which seem to show that, when the future is thought of at all, it is seen only in terms of its inconveniences. But why shirk at the thought that it could actually be quite different from what we have known? Why be afraid of asking those who already think differently from us? The Church and the religious life do not need dreamers or adventurers—but poets and, in the etymological sense of the word, creators: inventors and innovators, people with imagination, trained in history and having foresight. Renewal will be the work of the clearminded and courageous.

20. Quoted in *CTN* 39 (1966): 31.
21. "Fallait-il un Concile?" special no. of *La vie spirituelle* (Oct.-Nov. 1966), p. 276.

CHAPTER II

ST BERNARD'S IDEA OF THE ROLE
OF THE YOUNG[1]

FOR SOME TIME NOW the Church has had her
"youth movements," and they do not need any further
commendation from me. But the modern world has
youth movements, too, and they involve considerable agitation.
They are more or less to the fore in the different countries.
Some lay claim to power. In Christian society the problem of
how to treat the young and what opportunities to give them, is
quite real. There have been children's crusades, and history
shows that the Church often proves her vitality by the part
the young take in her activities. Does this sort of law apply
to monasticism? One of our great spiritual leaders, St Bernard of Clairvaux, who was alive to all the aspirations of a
period of renewal, has something to say about youth and the
young.

In the first place he recalled the theological principle inspired by Holy Scripture and by the whole of tradition: in itself
youth is no obstacle to the strong action of God on a human
person. In his treatise, *On the Conduct and Responsibility of
Bishops,* he protests against the abuse of raising children to
ecclesiastical dignity merely by reason of their noble birth,
and concludes: "Now I do not mean to say that any period
of life is too immature or too advanced to receive God's grace.
Many young people are more intelligent than the old, and
conduct themselves equally well. By virtue they are older
than their years, for their virtue makes up for what is lacking
to their age. There is real virtue in these children who seem to

1. *Collectanea Cisterciensia* 30 (1968): 120-127.

23

be children by age and yet strive to be good by abstaining from evil.[2] I say 'from evil' but not 'from sound judgment', it is precisely because they show sound judgment that no one may scorn them on account of their youth, as St Paul warns.[3] Upright children are much better than old people matured in evil."[4]

Many reminiscences of the Old and New Testament are recognisable here. St Bernard loved to dwell on this theme and drew inspiration also from the Book of Wisdom and the example of some of the young whom Scripture has praised: "Woe to the man of a hundred years if he is childish.[5] On the contrary if old age deserves respect this is not because of its many years.[6] The boy Samuel is a shining example. When the Lord spoke to him, he replied immediately 'Speak Lord, for your servant is listening,'[7] just as if he were using that verse of the psalm: 'I am not troubled, I am ready to fulfil your commands.'[8] Jeremiah is another shining example. He was sanctified before birth[9] and was established over peoples and over nations though he tried to avoid this on pretext of his youth. Then there was Daniel who by God's inspiration denounced an unjust judgment and thus saved the life of an innocent woman.[10] In a word, true grey hairs are qualities of the spirit and true old age is a life without blame.[11] When this type of youth, this kind of young man who is advanced in maturity, is promoted to some office, it is an intervention of God: those who do not resemble him and who cannot imitate him must at least admire him."[12]

It would be hard to show more confidence in youth. And

2. 1 Cor 14:20.
3. 1 Tim 4:12.
4. Dan 13:52.
5. Is 65:20.
6. Wis 4:8.
7. I Sam 3:10.
8. Ps 118:60 (Vulgate).
9. Jer 1:5-10.
10. Dan 15:45-62.
11. Wis 4:9.
12. *De moribus et officio episcoporum* 26; PL 182:826. The same distinction between the number of years and spiritual age is expressed in *Epist.* 254, 2-3; PL 182: 459-460.

what St Bernard affirmed in general and in principle, he illustrated by the example of one case in particular, that of St Malachy, Bishop of Armagh, whose life he wrote. As with many hagiographers, he was even more ignorant about his hero's youth, than about the rest of his life. And so, like many others, he had recourse to a theme that was spiritual rather than historical—that of early maturity spoken of in the Book of Wisdom. He says at the beginning: "His conduct was that of a mature person although he was still a child in years."[13] And a little further on, he speaks of his entrance into religious life: "Because he was so young, they thought he would be frivolous, they feared for his perseverance, for his constancy. Others accused him of being rash. They were indignant and annoyed at his precipitancy in embracing a way of life beyond the strength of his years. And yet he did nothing without taking advice,[14] and was well aware of those words of the Prophet: 'It is good for a man to bear the yoke from his youth'[15], and again: 'He will sit in solitude and silence for he knows how to forget himself.'[16] He sat long at the feet of Imar, a senior from whom he learned obedience, before he himself took to teaching. He grew strong in the habit of silence, knowing the Prohpet's word that silence is a way of doing good.[17] He remained within the enclosure and persevered. In this silence he would say to God with David: 'I am young and held in small esteem but I have not forgotten your commandments, O Lord!' "[18] Very soon he in his turn became a spiritual father. We recognize here the pattern of St Benedict's own life: less than three years after leaving Rome as a youth for the desert, he began to preach to the shepherds in the neighborhood and soon became a founder and an abbot. It is worth remembering that the Patriarch of the monks of the West instituted what has become the Benedictine way of life before he was twenty—according to St Gregory—and that St Bernard,

---

13. *Vita S. Malachiae* 1; *S. Bernardi opera* (Rome, 1963), 3:310.
14. Sir 32:24.
15. Lam 3:27.
16. Lam 3:28.
17. Is 32:17.
18. Ps 118:141 (Vulgate). *Vita S. Malachiae* 5; *S. Bernardi Opera*, 5:313-314.

who at twenty-two was a novice at Cîteaux, became Abbot of Clairvaux at twenty-five.

In Cistercian tradition, his youth was long remembered. It became a legend. A hundred years after his entrance into the monastery, in an account of the origins of the Cistercian Order, Conrad of Eberbach wrote: "The Lord raised up the spirit of a youth called Bernard. He was a delicate youth of noble birth and education. The fire of divine love burning within him was so strong that it caused him to abandon all the pleasures and riches the world could offer and ecclesiastical dignity as well, and take up the austere Cistercian life. He was like the first fruits of the Lord's harvest. Truly God is admirable in his works, and as the Psalmist says: "His word is swift: when he will he can show that what is impossible in the eyes of men is easy for him. The rich and noble, the middle classes, the poor, seeing the austerity of the Order, were all hesitant to join it, but he, for all his youth and delicacy, was animated by prevenient grace from the Lord's fount, inebriated with the wine that gladdens man's heart, and went about everywhere preaching the vocation. . . ."[19]

One of the last texts St Bernard produced carried an eulogy of youth. In the eighty-sixth *Sermon on the Song of Songs,* left unfinished at his death, he speaks of the reserve which should mark this time of life, and again quotes Jeremiah and the Psalmist: "It is good for man to bear the yoke from his youth. . . .[20] I am young and despised, but I have not forgotten your commandments, O Lord. . . ."[21] Earlier in the same work he had praised the generosity of youth in his commentary on the verse: "Your name is as oil poured out: therefore maidens have loved you exceedingly.[22] What comment can I make on this last word, *nimis*—exceedingly? It means very much, intensely, ardently." While on this point,

19. *Exordium magnum Cisterciense* d. 1, c. 21; ed. B. Griesser (Rome, 1961), p. 79.

20. Lam 3:27.

21. Ps 118:141 (Vulgate). *Sup. Cantica* 86, 2; *S. Bernardi Opera* (Rome, 1958) 2:318.

22. Song 1:2.

St Bernard recalls to balance and moderation the young monks
whom he is addressing. For while youth has its advantages
these very qualities present dangers, especially that of wanting
to go too far and do too much. "I am speaking especially to
you young people who have recently come to the cloister,"
he says. "For Scripture will have none of this extreme vehe-
mence that we sometimes experience and have to force ourselves to calm. It condemns your particular brand of intemper-
ance, your dissatisfaction with the ordinary observance: nothing satisfies you in our arrangements—whether they relate to
fasting, watches, manner of life, or the rules fixing the measure of food and type of clothing." He reminded them of
their model Jesus who, as a youth, told his parents that he
had to be busy about his Father's affairs. But when he saw
that they did not give in to him, he himself gave in and went
back to Nazareth with them: the Gospel simply says "he was
subject to them."[23] There must be order even in our ardor,
and self-possession, and free submission to God's demands,
as well as to those who guide us in his service, are the conditions for the purification of our faith and the growth of
our love, as St Bernard goes on to say. The entire sermon that
follows deals with this balancing of strength with sweetness
and courage with wisdom.

St Bernard had a good deal to do with the young, for many
came under his care. He seems to take real pleasure in ana-
lyzing their psychology. In another of the *Sermons on the
Song of Songs* he returns to the resourcefulness of youth—
and also its illusions. He shows that human nature is made for
giving itself, made for openness to the other, made for love;
and yet that each of us experiences the resistance that the
tendency to evil opposes to the inclination to the good. Adolescence is marked by an aggressiveness that must be controlled
with the help of grace. The Abbot of Clairvaux here shows
his basic optimism and realistic judgment. He trusts men, but
he knows men; he tries to mould them to the truth of their
nature, as created and recreated by God. Let us read again
this clear and balanced page. It is packed with biblical lyricism

23. 2:51. *Sup. Cantica* 19, 7; *S. Bern. Op.* (Rome, 1957), 1:112-113; CF 4:145.

which our own manner of thought and expression finds disconcerting. But the content is as topical for all times as is the problem that it endeavors to analyze:

Brotherly love is born in the deepest movements of the human heart. Man's true and inborn tenderness for his own self is like sap drawn from earth. It gives him the power of fertility, thus enabling him, with the help of grace, to produce the fruit of love. He will not consider it his duty to deny to the soul the fulfilment of the deepest longings of its very nature, but will even offer this same tenderness to one of his own nature acting thus whenever he can or needs to, in accord with a kind of natural law. When nature is not darkened by sin it shows this spirit of exquisite sweetness, experiencing and expressing tenderness rather than angry harshness toward fellow-sinners.

According to the Book of Wisdom, "dying flies spoil perfumed oil"[24] and nature has no power to remedy what it has lost. It knows that a dreadful metamorphosis drives it on down the slope, which Scripture so justly describes thus "The thoughts and feelings of a man are bent on evil from his youth."[25] The Gospel is not upholding a good youth when it shows us the younger son claiming his share of his inheritance. This claim involves the right to demand a division of a property that it would have been much better to hold in common; he wants for his own use a good that is not lessened by being held in common, and by the division he insists on, he causes the loss of his own share. Scripture tells us that he went through his money by living in debauchery with prostitutes. . . .[26] If the sinner is here shown to be the younger son it is because his nature, depraved by wantonness during a misguided adolescence, has lost all the vigor and wisdom of his manhood; his dry and loveless heart has hardened into contempt of all, and his only thought is for himself.

This is an example of how the thoughts and feelings of man are bent on evil from his very youth. Nature is moved to indignation rather than to pity. Man then, despoiled of his own humanity, seeks the aid of others in his need,

24. Eccles 10:1.
25. Gen 8:21.
26. LK 15:12-13.

though refusing them his own. Though he is a man himself, he judges other men with scorn and ridicule; though
a sinner himself he despises those who fall into sin, taking
no precautions against his own possible temptations,[27]
In this catastrophe, as I have said, nature has no power
to help herself. Once she has lost the oil of inborn
sweetness, she will not recover it. But grace can effect what nature cannot. If the unction of the Spirit
takes pity on a man and in this pity fills him again with his
sweetness, he will soon become a man again and in addition
will receive a better gift than he had from nature. It will
lead him to holiness in faith and love and will give him
not the oil but the balm of the vines of Engaddi.[28]

In this quotation, adolescence is really taken as a symbol
of nature left to itself and unable to fulfil itself without grace.
In accord with the whole line of tradition, St Bernard states
that Christian maturity is conferred by grace, not by age.
On the other hand, youth is not thereby guaranteed against
imprudence and error, and must be ready to accept the advice of another. St Bernard makes this last point clear in his
Third Sermon on Psalm Ninety, addressed to novices and
others whom he compares to new shoots: "You people are
like God's new seedlings.[29] So far, you have not trained your
senses to judge between good and evil[30]—so do not act on what
seems best to you. Do not be confident in your own judgment. . . ."[31] And he describes the illusions they are exposed
to, concluding: "Keep humble under God's mighty hand.[32]
He is your shepherd. Accept the advice of those who know
the devil's traps better than you do,[33] because experience has
taught them over a long period, both in themselves and in
many others."[34]

These doctrinal insights of St Bernard, found in his treatises

27. Gal 6:1.
28. Sir 45:4. *Sup. Cantica* 44, 4-6; *S. Bern. Op.,* 2:46-48.
29. Ps 148:12.
30. Heb 5:14.
31. Rom 14:5.
32. 1 Pet 5:6.
33. Cf. Gen 27:8.
34. *Super Ps., Qui habitat* 3:1; *S. Bern. Op.* (Rome, 1966). 4:393.

and sermons, throw light on his practical conduct as it manifests itself in his letters. To the abbot of St Victor in Paris he recommends a young cleric who has just arrived in the city to study; twenty years later this youth became its bishop. It was Peter Lombard.[35] Again, he sends a young man to the Pope, with a discreet word of praise for both his conduct and his culture—in the hope that help will be given him.[36] He is not afraid to trust and take a risk with the young who show themselves in any way trustworthy, even though they are still untried and untested by the experience which only life can give. For example, he writes to Pope Eugenius to commend a certain bishop: "This man has both youth and true dedication, *iuvenis devotus*. He needs the help of your fatherly encouragement. In the genuine and enlightened zeal he is showing for his Church, he must have not only your approval but your very real help, *sed et iuvandus*." In the play of words, *iuvenis —iuvandus*, we detect St Bernard's wit. And he concludes: "This help will make him more devoted, zealous and courageous!"[37]

One of Bernard's strongest points is that he could give such heart to young people who hesitated about following their monastic vocation. To a youth of great promise— *bonae spei iuveni*—as he called Thomas of Beverly, he addressed an exhortation to innocence of life. And if that is already tarnished by sins, even grievous sins, this need be no obstacle. In the words of the Psalm, Bernard held out the promise that "his youth would be renewed like the eagle's."[38] For another youth he cites a bit of Virgil, calling him a "handsome lad" *O formose puer!*—and putting him on his guard against the seductions to which his "tender age" exposes him. He recalls the example of the boy Jesus, who had the courage to withdraw sometimes from his kinsfolk and acquaintances.[39] We

35. *Epist.* 410; PL 182:618-619. The letter dates from 1139. Peter Lombard became bishop of Paris in 1159. He was born shortly after 1100.

36. In *Études sur S. Bernard et le texte de ses écrits* (Rome, 1953), p. 96, I have published this text.

37. *Epist.* 278; PL 182:484.

38. *Epist.* 411; PL 182:619. Cf. Ps 102:5 (Vulgate). Epistle 2 (PL 182:79) begins with this address "To the young man Fulco of good disposition."

39. *Epist.* 412; PL 182:620, quotes Virgil, *Ecl.* 2:17.

find an entire letter to the countess of Blois defending her
son, who had committed some "excess." Bernard does not
name it except to say that it is "excusable in an adolescent."
"The mature owe it to the young to overlook their misdeeds
for they themselves have acted similarly at the same age."
The young deserve our understanding and our trust as well
as the chance to prove their mettle; they need not only our
help, but the proof of our love. Sympathetic understanding
will go much further than anger or pointed reproof. "Your
idea is that your son has not treated you as he should. And
yet, in my opinion his conduct has been perfect. If he acts
toward all as he has toward me, then I am more than satisfied."[40] It was a discreet lesson for the Countess of Blois—and
stands for us as clear proof of the way in which the Abbot of
Clairvaux could handle the young.

* * * * *

In a sermon on St Bernard preached at the beginning of the
thirteenth century, Phillip, Chancellor of the University of
Paris, declared that there are two kinds of youth—and that
each has its own way of celebrating.[41] Some use tam-
bourines, harps and noisy organs to accompany them.
Others delight in interior renewal, and this kind of youth
is inexhaustible. It is renewed like the eagle and is the
beginning of that everlasting vitality of which the Prophet
Osee had a foretaste in his youth,[42] and which was revealed
to the author of the Apocalypse when he heard harps in
heaven accompanying the canticle of God's servant, Moses,
and the canticle of the Lamb.[43] "To sing for God is nothing
else than to thank him" for this sharing in the youth of God
which is communicated to men in the victory of Christ. And
yet, youth remains an age of mystery. For the Chancellor of
the University of Paris as for the author of Proverbs, whom
he quotes, "The way of the young is difficult to compre-

40. *Epist.* 300; PL 182:502. Bernard also says with reference to youthful
follies of a recently nominated bishop: "Why are the youthful follies of a young
man like this still remembered? These former things have passed away."

41. Under the title "Sermon de Philippe le Chancelier sur S. Bernard" in *Citeaux*
16 (1965): 205-213, I have published this text.

42. Hos 2:15.

43. Rev 15:2-3.

hend."[44] It is like sparkling new wine already rich in its content but not clarified.

This educator was well acquainted with the young and with Bernard's way of treating them. For his part, Bernard had only conformed his outlook to an idea expressed by St Benedict. In this regard the author of the Rule had given proof of his trust in the Holy Spirit and his enlightened charity—two qualities that are likely to be weakened in institutions. In the chapter on calling the brethren to council on important matters he tells the abbot to ask the advice of all "for the Lord often reveals to the younger what is best."[45] And this is not only in extraordinary circumstances but a regular thing: *saepe*; and for all young people without restriction—*juniori*. Elsewhere he refers to Samuel and Daniel, who as children judged the elder.[46]

Why this respect for the young? Why this trust that the Holy Spirit will speak through them? Is his aim here not to remind us all that those good ideas we get for the conduct of our own Christian life are always a revelation from God himself: *Dominus revelat*. This is a lesson in humility and supernatural outlook. Because we are adults—on in years, some of us, and enriched with much human experience, we are inclined to think that our maturity is the source of our useful thoughts. St Benedict reminds us that in all that concerns salvation and the means that lead to God, because these come from his in the first place, nothing happens except by inspiration, through a "revelation" of what is hidden from our senses and our reason. These two may even act as a screen, and stand like obstacles between God's action and our response.

It is good for us to be reminded of our limitations and to hold suspect all natural opinions. Practical commonsense, moderation, sound judgment and all those human qualities we find often come in for praise in the Rule. They are not to be denied. But they did not deter the Saint from writing this disconcerting formula: "The Lord often reveals to the younger what is best." We should weigh well every word of this.

44. Prov 30:18.
45. *Rule of St. Benedict*, ch. 3:3.
46. *Ibid.*, ch. 63:6.

CHAPTER III

SEPARATION FROM THE WORLD AND RELATIONS WITH THE WORLD

THIS IS A DOUBLE PROBLEM, and we need to know what factors in it are constants as they stand out in monastic tradition. Moreover, for an accurate assessment of the past we must consider the present as well, for the present has made its own assessment of the past and taken its own orientations toward the future, and so it forms part of "contemporary" history as we call it.

History offers an abundance of material in every succeeding epoch which we may classify in two categories: facts and ideas.

FACTS

Monasticism has always involved separation from the world—not only from the carnal and sinful element in any given age and epoch, but from ordinary society as well, even from ordinary Christian society; and it has involved relationships with the world. To consider only one of these aspects, to over-stress either of them is to risk missing the balance and complementarity existing between them. In itself this balance is the unchangeable factor, whereas this or that actual realization strongly stressing one or other aspect, is the exception, even though a legitimate one.

SEPARATION FROM THE WORLD

This has always been *real*, in the sense of physical and material: not merely a spiritual attitude or disposition of the

33

heart, like detachment from the sinful world and awareness of being "not of the world" which are common to all Christians.

This separation from the world has been determined by the "search for God"—a quest that results in detachment from everything in the world that can turn one away from God—that is, from sin—and everything that distracts the attention from God. The goal of seeking God prompts some souls to withdraw from ordinary social life and, in this sense, to flee. Under this aspect every monk goes into solitude. He is a solitary in relation to the world.

But where is this solitude found? In what place do we seek it? It makes no difference where, provided that the conditions just indicated are fulfilled. In the country, perhaps. Rural solitude has been certainly the most usual for monasteries, although in the first centuries there were virgins and ascetics who lived at home in the city. Rural solitude was the original choice of many monasteries which later found themselves in towns or became towns themselves. The "desert" did not have to be a long way from the city—recall the "desert" of Port Royal and of the nearby Abbey of Vaux des Cernay. But is was always a place apart—*in locum seorsum.*

There were urban monasteries, plenty of them. Or rather, monasteries which were originally founded on the outskirts of cities, in the suburbs, near the churches close to the city gates or walls where there were cemeteries or the tombs of martyrs and confessors. We have only to think of St Germain des Pres, St Maur des Fosses, Saint Martin in the fields, Saint Paul outside the walls. A number of monasteries that were founded in the country gave rise to monastic villages—like that of Cluny which is still standing today.[1] In both of these cases, from the beginning or soon after, a system of urban enclosure was found necessary. This was the way some of the Cluniac regulations governing enclosure arose. City monasteries were not just country monasteries transplanted—nor

1. These monastic towns have been studied by E. Lesne, *Histoire de la propriété ecclésiastique en France. VI: Les églises et les monastères, centres d'accueil, d'exploitation et de peuplement* (Lille, 1943), pp. 389-399.

were the conditions found in these city monasteries applicable without change to the country. Suppleness and variety of institutions ought to allow for adaptation to the conditions of each site.

But *how* was separation from the world to be assured? By *enclosure* as a basic observance, for it is both the sign and the guarantee of monastic solitude. But enclosure was not seclusion, even for nuns—except for the men and women recluses who sometimes lived in monasteries or close by. For the individual, flexibility of enclosure allowed for trips and travel; we shall consider this matter further on, under the heading of relations with the world. For the individual, too, flexibility of enclosure also allowed for eremitical life—whether in one place or as a pilgrim, whether permanent or temporary—and also in some cases, for preaching. As for communities, the law of enclosure did not forbid nuns from going out: nor did it forbid others—clerics or laity, men or women—from coming in, for purposes considered reasonable by the abbes. This held good even after the decretal *Periculoso* of Boniface VIII (1298) and even after the Council of Trent. It was certainly true of Saint-Sauveur at Nimes and Saint-Pierre-les-Nonnains at Lyons.[2] Other examples could be cited.

But while the fact of enclosure does not vary, the forms in which this observance was expressed have differed greatly: from the recluses' wall and the nuns' grille, to Charles de Foucauld's row of stones, or a simple agreement, as in the United States, or just the sign: "Private."

The *purpose* and *result* of this separation from the world is recollection—and sometimes a safeguard against one's self. To the observance of enclosure should be added conditions favoring peace and prayer. These have been adapted to every type of civilization—according to time and place; they have not been artificial imitations of other periods or systems. But the constant element has always been silence which was regarded as constituting a personal enclosure within the common enclosure for each one in the community.

2. I hope to publish some documents that I have on these two monasteries.

The *foundation* of this separation from the world was the existence of a spirituality of monastic solitude: faith in the value of contemplative search for God, acceptance of the detachment inherent in exile, *exodus,* desert, renunciation. The Lord had made his call clear to some—and they are exemplified by Abraham, the Apostles and St Anthony. We are not attempting to explain this spirituality here, this will be done later,[3] but only to stress the fact that separation is not an observance without the backing of spiritual doctrine, without justification. Quite the contrary, monastic "faith" tends to concretize itself in *praxis.*

In the same way, stability was not presented as forbidding exits or contacts with the world, but as an inner need of the monk. The realization of this need supposes discernment, spiritual perception and charity—in the monk just as much as in his abbot.

RELATIONS WITH THE WORLD

Relations with the world have always existed in the monastic life—even for men and women recluses. They are necessitated by the very nature of man as being in relation. They constitute an integral part of the search for God. Such relationship with the world carries the risks and weaknesses inherent in every human institution. Dangers have not always been avoided, even the window of the recluse occasioned some abuses.

WHAT WAS THE FORM OF THIS RELATIONSHIP WITH THE WORLD

Openness. Persons and ideas were accepted, welcomed and invited. Assistance in spiritual need was the second form of monastic openness, and it tended to predominate over the first (in seventeenth and nineteenth century Europe, for example). The ascendancy of this latter form was brought about through the development of different types of charitable

3. See below, ch. 5.

and social aid, by the added requirement of priesthood for monks and by the closer identification of the office of spiritual director with the exercise of priesthood.

Many monasteries gathered round them a kind of coterie, flexible and varied in type and in numbers. The material bond here would be the fixed meeting place, fitting the changing conditions of different periods, like the medieval hostelries for rich and for poor. The spiritual or juridical bond conformed to the different types of social relationship, feudal or otherwise. The coterie attached to Saint-Germain-des-Pres provides a good example of this type of influence in the Maurist period as well as in the medieval.[4] The growth of this type of contact is often seen in correspondence emerging from business, friendship and counsel, as we can see from the many letters of consolation and direction. This bulk of correspondence is relatively larger in monastic circles than elsewhere, if we can judge by the documents that have been preserved.

But there was openness not only to people but also to the *ideas* current in the culture of every period; the humanistic culture of the High Middle Ages, the scholastic from the twelfth century onward (as evidenced by the library of Mont-Saint-Michel[5] or of Clairvaux),[6] the scientific trends (erudite and otherwise) of the Maurists and others, the religious currents of the seventeenth and eighteenth centuries including the Jansenism of so many of the Maurists and Vannists and the influence of freemasonry at Fleury and elsewhere, and of the nineteenth century, especially of ultramontanism. In general, this openness to the current culture reflects zeal: there has been a spontaneous though not always enlightened veering toward whatever could foster the search for God even indirectly and toward the broad, absolute and radical forms of the religious aspirations proper to every period and country.

4. I have made a study of this example in *Aux sources de la spiritualité occidentale* (Paris, 1964), pp. 255-267.

5. I have given examples under the title "Une bibliothèque vivante" in *Millénaire monastique du Mont-Saint-Michel* (Paris, 1967), 2:247-255.

6. Cf. A. Wilmart, "L'ancienne bibliothèque de Clairvaux" in *Mémoirs de la Société académique . . . de l'Aube* 81 (1917): 125-190.

Relationship with the world has always been bound up with *work*. The type of relationship and the kind of people with whom the monks were in contact through their work has varied with the type of work itself. So we have the *Rule of St Benedict* describing crafts as normal and field labor as exceptional. Later on, there were the relationships with the workmen in the monastic villages, and with the country folk in their rural dependencies. The Cistercians are exceptional for they usually adopted a livelihood connected with some type of farming. It is clear that the importance and technical character of work in the second half of the twentieth century differs greatly from that of the nineteenth—but the constant factor is that if monks work, then by the very fact and to the extent of the work, they cannot avoid relations with the world of work.

Legislation has always regarded *trips* and *travel* as necessary but also as subject to the control of regulations. While the *Rule of St Benedict* makes only one allusion to the danger of leaving the monastery without need (ch. 66: "for this is by no means expedient for their souls"), it devotes three chapters (60, 61 and 67) to the brethren on a journey. In fact, there has always been need for some monks to travel. We find them on pilgrimage or on business—dealing with distant property or legal actions or settling disputes. All these situations involve personal encounters. There were cultural exchanges too—involving journeys to copy manuscripts and do various types of research. There were friendly visits[7] and involvement in ecclesiastical or secular affairs, as, for example, with Jean de Gorze in Andalusia,[8] the Cluniac abbots in Italy and Spain,[9] St Bernard in several European countries, and many others. Originally monks would go out for the celebration of the Eucharist. Later, when the sacraments were administered in monasteries, these still remained the occasion for contact between monks and the people, both clergy and laity,

7. I have quoted examples under the titles "Les relations entre le monachisme oriental et le monachisme occidental dans le haut moyen âge" in *Millénaire du Mont-Athos* (Chevetogne, 1965), 2:56-70.

8. Cf. *Aspects du monachisme hier et aujourd hui* (Paris, 1968), pp. 248-257. [ET: CS 7].

9. Cf. *Ibid.*, pp. 215-231.

either inside the enclosure, or outside, in the circumstances mentioned above, leading naturally to conversation and mutual changes of advice and encouragement.

These relations with the world were so many forms of *sharing both spiritual and material* goods flowing from the monastic solitude: the loan and dispatch of manuscripts, contact with pilgrims or visitors to the monastery; small schools inside the enclosure, and outside, sometimes—at a later period—staffed by monks rather than by seculars; occasional preaching in churches, as at Cluny; the missionary activity of some monks —but a very different thing from the later developments of the sixteenth and especially the nineteenth centuries and the gradual, in fact rather slow, increase of the priesthood. This increase of the priesthood has entailed more contact with the world than previously, and in many countries such contact has taken a course that is not in line with monasticism.

With this and other types of development it is necessary to maintain that such recent facts, even though numerous—even if today they have become more or less general, do not constitute a constant element in monasticism, and they give no definite orientation to the future. The genuine monastic charism must distinguish, recover, and restore the "permanent values." For example, if the recruitment policy of communities of monks is based on aptitude for clerical studies and the priesthood, it is thereby a selection determined by a standard of previous education, and so is actually restricted to a certain economic level. This is quite a recent phenomenon, still in process of evolution—and so it is not to be taken as normative.

In the same way, abbots have become involved in certain relations with a certain section of the world by receiving pontifical insignia and titles and prelacies. "They insist on being called barons," said a fourteenth-century monk.[10] We have only to think of the title, "Lord Abbot," in the sense that the word "Lord" was given in England and Ireland until

10. "Vocant se etiam barones": Monastic letter of the fourteenth century, which I published under the title "Pour l'histoire de l'obéissance au moyen âge" in *Revue d'ascétique et de mystique* 12 (1965): 128.

the Reformation. One of the reasons most often brought forward today for the suppression of these titles and insignia is to put an end to this wordly element that has been introduced into the very core, the very center of the institution, and consequently in the very heart of monks themselves as persons. This prelacy of abbots is not a constant in monasticism. Whatever be its origins and early forms,[11] it is, in so far as it sought to make abbots like bishops, really a later accretion, often appearing in periods of decadence.

As a final thought on separation from the world, it must be remembered that relationship with the world demands *real spirituality as its basis*: a true appreciation of the place of monasticism in the Church as a mystery of charity and universal solidarity, and a deep experience of that communion which the cenobite finds in community. History shows that this radiance of charity existed and remains strong in monasticism only in proportion as the monks have been men of solitude and men of community, for the charity which needs and feeds their search for God expands and expresses itself in their mutual understanding. Even hermits, who withdraw from these communities yet remain united to them, are one of the manifestations of the radiance of charity shed by them.

CONCLUSIONS

Relating to both separation from the world and relations with the world, history shows that institutions were flexible at the beginning—having all the risks inherent in liberty. One of the constant elements has been a hardening process in institutions overcoming this original flexibility, especially when there was no spirituality animating the observances. Instead of conviction, we have laws that become increasingly precise and unlikely to engender convictions of a new and perhaps nobler kind. Thus the enclosure of nuns has been punctiliously regulated in periods of decadence to remedy abuses of a previous period, and these punctilious regulations eventually became

11. Cf. P. Salmon, *Etudes sur les insignes du pontife dans le rite romain. Histoire et liturgie* (Rome, 1955).

the norm for every time and place, every type of civilization and religious life.

Though separated from the world, the monastery has always had its relationship with it, such as it is found in every state of society, with its structures, its forms of economy, its culture, its political organization—the temporal element aiding and protecting, or exploiting and hindering according to the circumstances.[12] When the structure of society was Christian or at least recognized the Church, monasticism related quite naturally, both by separation and union, with the whole society and with all its members of every class, rich and poor. However, its recruiting strength lay largely with the well-to-do.[13] The institution of lay religious as a separate class does not weaken this fact; for this institution arose with Cîteaux, and was adopted by traditional monasticism recently;[14] it is now on the way out, and constitutes a parenthesis rather than a constant.

From the nineteenth century monasteries remained completely apart; it was then, as Pius XI said, that "the Church lost the working classes"—though this is only one instance of the ruptures effected at that time. The principal relationship of monasticism was with those who were the proprietory class—with those who controlled either the economic or cultural values. It no longer had relations with society as a whole but with that part of it which was still Christian. During this period priesthood became general for all who were not lay brothers. There were accompanying consequences in the area of recruitment and formation, and this factor contributed considerable to giving monasticism a touch of aristrocracy both bourgeois and clerical. But these recent historical developments are not constants. If the Church and society are

12. Cf. *Aspects du monachisme*, pp. 279-294.
13. For the Middle Ages see G. Penco, "La composizione sociale delle communità monastiche nei primi secoli" in *Studia Monastica* 4 (1962): 257-281.
14. J. Dubois, "L'institution des convers au XIIe siècle, forme de vie monastique propre aux laïcs," in *I laici nella "Societas christiana" dei secoli XI e XII* (Milan, 1968), pp. 183-261. Under the title "Comment vivaient les frères convers" in the same volume, pp. 152-176, and in *Analecta Cisterciensia* 21 (1965): 239-258, I have quoted evidence especially from Cistercian history.

evolving during this second half of the twentieth century, surely monasticism has no obligation to retain the mentality and structures of the previous era. On every level in the technical world—from advanced research to manual labor—a new type of humanism is appearing. The constant elements which have marked the whole of monastic history, separation from the world and relations with it, must be balanced with this new type of humanism, as with everything else. Monks might well have much to learn from technicians—even if only from the earnestness of their research. If you visit an atomic research center you come away with the strong impression that the men live there like monks—in solitude, silence and work, in the sole presence of the object of their quest. But they often lack a "beyond," whereas monasticism points to it.

In a secularized world monasticism has two duties in regard to the forms it employs to express its relationships. First, it must eliminate forms not understood by the world, or surprise it, or give offence without adequate reason. Secondly, monasticism should adopt those forms or relationships which are more expressive in the world of today, such as working for one's living. Separation can be fully maintained without having to be expressed in repulsive forms.

IDEAS

As for monastic doctrine, many ideas could be put forward, and many texts cited. It will be enough for our present purpose to point out the constants, in relation to which today's problems, new or renewed, are posed, and which show in which direction the solutions lie.

Separation from the world. Until the present day, within the Church monks and others have regarded separation from the world as *a normal state in the Christian life*—one that is simply taken for granted and has no need to be justified, legitimized or, still less, excused. But today, even Christians seem to regard it as a form of betrayal and they are posing a question which monks have no right to avoid.

The answer is found in certain elements of the spiritual

tradition which are constant and complementary, but between which we must distinguish more precisely in the present day. On the one hand, the Gospel calls men to a "spiritual" break with the world in so far as it is carnal, that is, sinful. Let us take this detachment, this withdrawal as the formal element in separation from the world. But not being "of the world" does not mean not being "in the world." All Christians, even monks, are "not of the world" (and in this sense out of the world), while at the same time "in the world." But from the very beginning and with the approval of the Church, some have added material separation to this formal separation: they have expressed and signified the formal by the material. And they have done it for motives which they called evangelical. But in explaining and justifying their conduct they have not always distinguished carefully the two aspects, and have sometimes even insisted on the second (that is, material separation) in such a way as to give the impression that this was in fact primary, whereas it is really only a means and a symbol of spiritual separation. And yet there is no lack of evidence in favor of their love of neighbor and their sense of universal solidarity: they have chosen to serve and to love through withdrawal.

Yet most of the old evidence in favor of this attitude shows that the world one withdraws from was regarded under a somewhat static aspect, this is, as including two elements standing in permanent opposition, as if this were final and the elements themselves forever irreconcilable. Today, many see this opposition between the world and God as a question rather badly expressed, so that its solution needs to be reconsidered, and perhaps revised, at least in its presentation and expression. This opinion is widely held even outside the Teilhardian school of thought. The result will be a better evaluation of *all* the constants in tradition, with clearer distinctions between them.

Today the world presents itself as a dynamic and evolving reality, progressing by means of man's collaboration with God. Traces of the influence of this idea can be found in *Gaudium et Spes*. "Development" of the world is no longer viewed simply as a consequence or reward, as it was in the economy of monasticism; it is something sought, as is clear in the encyclical *Populorum Progressio*. What was formerly considered to be in opposition is now seen in a different light; there is a kind of fusion, or else confusion. What value is retained then by separation from the world and the expressions that monasticism has given to it? They remain legitimate only if separation is placed on its true level—which is not the level of appearances, or of the earthly and visible or material element which it requires, but rather, of the spiritual element of inner reality. "Be solitaries, but in soul, not in body. Be solitaries by the orientation of your heart, the gift of your life to God. Be solitaries in an interior way. For Christ the Lord, who is Spirit, demands solitude of soul and not solitude of the body," says St Bernard, and many others with him.[15] Exterior, material separation must always be controlled by reference to what the world is in each different period and type of civilization, and by the formal interior element of solitude.

As to the vocabulary of "separation" from the world, it represents a constant only in so far as it is bound up with New Testament terminology. Every epoch right up till our own has had its characteristic approach, its own vision of the world—and this characteristic approach has left its mark on the form of separation. If this attitude toward the world is evolving under the guidance of the Church, for example, under the influence of the Constitution *Gaudium et Spes* from Vatican II, then vocabulary and presentation may be modified without compromising the inner reality—the formal element—as expressed in the New Testament.

This distinction between the formal element and the material, and the proper relationship between them makes monks wonder if they have in fact reversed the values—and therefore makes them criticize their own attitude. From this sifting, some are drawing the conclusion that the material ele-

15. *Sup. Cantica* 40, 4; *S. Bernardi Opera*, 2: 27; earlier in the same sense, St Basil, *Epist.* 2; PG 32: 224-225.
16. P. Evdokimov, *Les âges de la vie spirituelle* (Paris, 1964), p. 121.
17. Cf. *Aspects du monachisme*, pp. 118-123.

ment has in fact lost its force: physical, material separation must give way to an "interiorised monasticism," in the words of Evdokimov.[16] On the other hand, we have people in the world showing great regard for monastic solitude, and experiencing the need for it.[17] So in the face of a concrete provocation, at once physical and real, by which the world continues to flood the heart of man with tumult and dissipation, a concrete separation is legitimate, if it is directed to the search for God in inner peace.

CONCLUSION

The spiritual constants of earlier centuries remain viable. But monks today must undertake an honest self-examination about these spiritual and institutional constants. But does not the material element come to the fore? Do we not tend to make a screen of it, hiding the fact that the formal element is either lacking or on the decline? Do we not tend to turn it into a work of salvation that is efficacious in itself— or else a factor contributing to our superiority, more or less conscious and avowed? Physical, exterior separation from the world is really our practical expression of an interior attitude —the detachment of the heart for union with God. Do our relations with the world bear the clear mark of charity and humility, of a Christian reading of the signs of the times, of consent to the work of God which is being carried on in the world and the Church of today?

CHAPTER IV

SOLITARY LIFE AND COMMON LIFE

O NE OF THE SIGNS OF RENEWAL in the contemplative life today is the fact that Christian men and women are taking up the solitary or eremitical life. Some of these are living independently, while others are connected with a monastery, i.e., with monks and nuns who follow the common or cenobitic life.[1]

Admittedly, it is difficult to present the issue accurately. There has been, and still is, a good deal said and written about the respective advantage of the eremitic life and the cenobitic, about the superiority of one over the other and about the connection between them. Some stress their difference, to indicate their mutual incompatibility: others stress their similarity. The wiser course, however, is to keep to the facts. These are complex and varied,[2] and we merely summarize them briefly here.[3]

IN THE EAST

It is a mistake to think that the cenobitic life sprang from the eremitic, or vice versa. Rules, clear-cut forms and struc-

1. An indication of this fact is that there have been already published two articles in the review edited under the supervision of the Congregation of Religious *Vita religiosa* 3 (1967): M. Farrel, "Attualità della vita eremitica," pp. 29-40 and J. Leclercq, "L'eremitismo ieri et oggi," pp. 243-252.

2. See the two excellent articles of C. Lialine, "Eremitisme en Orient" and of P. Doyère, "Eremitisme en Occident" in *Dictionnaire de spiritualité* 6:1 (1960), col. 936-982.

3. For the first part concerning the East, I have been assisted by the erudition of P. J. Gribomont OSB to whom I tender grateful thanks.

tures—all these represent a second phase in monastic history. The monastic life derives from the asceticism of the early Church, or rather from the Christianity of the Gospels. It is an attempt to express its radical fulfillment, an attempt to live a *perfect* or *apostolic* or *heavenly* life. The first really successful attempts are those that have a rule and imply a discipline: this is the point of contrast with the unsuccessful experiments. But historically, the first monks were the sarabites, who had neither rule nor superior. Eremitic and cenobitic life have both derived from this, each in its own way.

Lower Egypt, with its lauras or eremitical colonies, offers the finest examples of eremitic life. A similar though more mobile type of life seems to predominate in the Syrian region to the north and the east. In contrast with this, we find Pachomius and Basil linking perfection very closely with common life. In literary prestige, eremitism soon ranked very high. Through Jerome, Rufinus and others, it spread to the West.

Eremitism is more striking. It seems to give deeper expression to that impulse in monasticism which refuses to be satisfied with an ecclesiastical expression of Christian living, and attempts to create a new style of life. Pachomius and Basil, on the other hand and independently of each other, tend to identify their community with the local Church.

The Greek monasticism deriving from this did not stress these differences, which arose from actual situations rather than from theological conclusions. Pachomius and Basil felt from their own experience that those who refused to join a community or who later sought a more withdrawn life were not well motivated, and were taking a risky step. One gets the impression that in this matter the saints were more flexible in deed than in word.

The Eastern type of monasticism, which took shape in Palestine at the beginning of the fifth century, combined the normal cenobitical life required of the beginners with the eremitical freedom reserved for the proficient. This seems to be the solution foreshadowed by Cassian, according to the mind of St Benedict.

Absence of cenobitic discipline can result in many abuses; from time to time there are reactions of the Basilian type: that of Theodore the Studite is one such example. But this isolation does not last. Not only in Russia but in Byzantium also, with Simeon the New Theologian, the Studites quickly gave place to the eremitic ideal praised so highly in the "Lives of the Desert Fathers." Even though Athos is structured round communities, the Eastern ideal still centers on the hermit. The writings of Basil are less popular than those of the Hesycasts.

Usually only the permission of the Higoumene[4] was required when one wanted to leave the community. Many texts show that eremitic vocations were discouraged for a period long enough to constitute a severe test.

IN THE WEST

If one examines a great number of documents that give practical proof of the principle here enunciated, it is clear that, in the West, three periods are to be distinguished:[5] the first and longest stretched from the beginnings of the cenobitic life right up to modern times. During this period a stable monastic tradition is recognizable. A second and shorter period stretches from the beginnings of the sixteenth to the middle of the twentieth century. This may be treated as a parenthesis. Finally, we note a third period, beginning about 1940-45 and bringing a move to revive the authentic tradition. These periods need to be dealt with one at a time.

TRADITIONAL MONASTICISM

The constants in the expression of the eremitic ideal are embodied in a structure and in various elements.

Essentially, the structure consists in the fact that from

4. Cf. P. de Meester, *De monachico statu iuxta disciplinam byzantinam,* (Rome, 1942) paragraph 126, with the indication of documents.

5. In a series of studies, the bibliographical indications of which are given in *Vita religiosa, art. cit.,* I have quoted texts and facts and given references; these documentary contributions will be taken for granted in the present exposition.

earliest times Church legislation allows that some monks should withdraw to live in hermitage with the permission of their abbot, under his direction and close to the monastery itself. Thus in 465 the Council of Vannes issued a Canon on this matter.[6] It is clear from this text that the monk leaving the community to live apart from, though still connected with it, need not necessarily be motivated by the fact that he is strong enough to do without it. His own weakness, inability to withstand the difficulties of common observance, even physical infirmities are also accepted as reasons. Other texts of the same period make this abundantly clear.[7]

Evidence of the reality of the eremitical vocation occupies a considerable place in recent studies of Benedictine historiography. The facts are not less striking. "In withdrawing some distance from their monasteries," one writer says, "those who were authorized to live as hermits were still under the immediate direction of their abbot. It is no mere coincidence then, that close to the old abbeys, and their dependencies, one finds a certain number of hermitages. In periods of fervor these would always be occupied by religious in search of greater perfection."[8] Moreover, many monastic charters indicate privileges granted to such-and-such an abbey "and its hermitages." Specific mention is made of hermits in many chronicles and necrologies. Other more explicit literary sources, including the *Lives* of saints give examples of these supernatural gifts and help us to understand both the ideal which attracted them

6. "It is prescribed also for monks that they may not leave the community for solitary cells, unless they have deserved it by meritorious deeds or the severity of the rule is relaxed because of weak health. Finally it may be that they remain within the enclosure of the monastery under the jurisdiction of the Abbot, but living in cells apart from the community." This text is given as that of the Council of Vannes (465) (Mansi 7:954) in I. I. Gavigan, *De Vita Monastica in Africa Septentrionali* (Turin, 1962), p. 136; as to the Council of Agde (526) see C. Capelle, *Le voeu d'obéissance des origines au XIIᵉ siècle* (Paris, 1959), p. 80, no. 39.

7. Also the "Paenitentiale Cummeani" (506): "It is better for you if in weak health to lead a solitary life, than to perish with the crowd." quoted in *Zeitschrift für katholische Theologie* (1963), p. 420, where there is likewise reproduced this passage from the Rule of Columkille: "Be alone in a separate place near a chief city, if your conscience is not sufficiently prepared to be in common with the crowd."

8. J. de Trévilliers, *Sequania monastica* (Vesoul, s. d. [1955]) 2:101.

and the status of those who sought to realize this ideal. The significant characteristic is that the hermits remained dependent on a monastery: usually they lived close to it, and remained under the direction of the abbot. In this way, they did not deviate either from the law of obedience or from that of stability. They received help from their brethren, and sometimes gave help in return. Those who left the monastery in this way were those whose fervor needed more "freedom" for prayer and penance than the common observance allowed. In cases like this, it is stated specifically that the monk "chose to retire to the desert in order to follow his call to austerity, not wanting his own singularity to be a cause of disquiet to the weak."[9]

Among hermits of this kind were to be found monks, abbots and bishops who had once been monks and had retired from the episcopacy. The degree of seclusion varied from that of the recluse to that of the quasi-hermit who remained in the monastery and was dispensed from part or all of the common observance. Mention should also be made of those monks who lived in a grange or priory, alone or with one or two companions, coming to the monastery from time to time to take part in the office. At Cluny and its dependencies there was, as at Athos a certain degree of monastic pluralism. Traditional monasticism—known in the twelfth century as "black" to distinguish in from the new or reformed monasticism of the Cistercians—has always been able to preserve a degree of flexibility in its structures. In the tenth century, Sicily and Calabria even saw a purely Eastern form of the eremitical ideal.

Some hermits remained settled for a long time in one place. Others had none of this stability. They would be wanderers, in the traditional sense of the word *peregrinatio*, which indicates voluntary exile rather than the notion of a pilgrimage or visit to some shrine. A kind of dialectical necessity would force the hermit to change his abode: his life of prayer and penance would have an influence on others, who would be drawn to

9. *Vita S. Jacobi Eremitae* 21, ed. Mabillon, *Acta sanctorum OSB*, 4:11 (Paris, 1680), p. 151.

visit him, and in the end, disciples would want to live with him. If he really wanted to follow his own vocation he would be forced to seek solitude elsewhere. Frequent and almost normal instability was the lot of the medieval hermit—perhaps of all hermits at any time. The same reasons which caused instability of domicile would also cause variety in the duration of the eremitic call: for some the call would be permanent, for others it might be temporary. It might be a phase at the beginning of conversion, preparing for the cenobitic life, or it might come as the crown of a life in community. It might also happen that periods of solitude would alternate with periods in the cenobium. Finally, there are many instances of monks seeking solitude in groups. Here again there is a range of possibilities from the floating hermitages *in deserto oceani* to wandering or stable groups on some continent. "One of the characteristics of medieval eremiticism was that it was rarely individual."[10] Very often the hermit would find himself at the head of a group of companions, a kind of colony. This laura type of eremitic life was possibly the outcome of an evolution; it came into being when the solitary ceased to be isolated, but at the same time had no urge to establish a cenobium properly so called; he established his disciples about him organizing their life in hermitages similar to his own. This would involve only a few, and each continued to live in solitude as a hermit. The characteristic constants of eremitical life show up clearly in relation to cenobitism.

In a very general way one might say that eremitism is the exception in the monastic life: the hermit goes further than others; he goes as far as possible in that search for solitude with God which is traditionally held to be the end of the monastic vocation. This kind of need to press onwards to the very limit characterizes his ideal, even when his expression of it falls short. In fact, the documents warrant the statement that the traits proper to the eremitic life result from its thrust toward deeper solitude, more prayer and greater asceticism.

First, *deeper solitude*. The context of the eremitic life is the

10. J. de Trévilliers, *op. cit.,* p. 101.

desert; it must be sufficiently large to isolate one who withdraws there, and sufficiently uncultivated to be in no way attractive to others who might come there to seek an easy life, and so, by that very fact, put an end to the solitude. This isolation is often found in a forest. As for the dwelling itself, it was distinctive by reason of its small size: only a hut or a shed.

The true hermit is sociable and social. He needs to meet other human beings from time to time. The remote and inconvenient nature of the place where he lives gives him sometimes an opportunity of offering hospitality to those who happen to pass his way. He does not refuse to have an influence on others, even if this should assume the proportions of an apostolate.

If these monks want more solitude than others, it is in order to have *more prayer*: the prayer of the hermit is more continuous, simpler and less varied in form than prayer life in community. It is based largely on the psalms; the psalter is the sum total of the hermit's goods.

Finally, unless he is ill, the hermit has come to the desert for *stricter discipline* and *greater austerity*. The need for penance finds expression first of all in work, the manual labor that is more indispensable for him than for the cenobite; he is in need of the fruits or vegetables he is growing; moreover, he is working the soil as a means of mortification and in order to procure the wherewithal for almsgiving. The hermit's intellectual development is certainly affected by this; as a result the eremitical life is not strongly intellectual in character. Finally, in a phrase inspired by St Jerome, the hermit goes out into the desert naked, that is to say in the spirit of interior despoliation and exterior destitution. The habit he assumes is simple, rough, comfortless, and witnesses to both poverty and austerity.

THE MODERN PARENTHESIS

Influenced doubtless by the strengthing of ecclesiastical legislation and by a certain structural rigidity which followed the Council of Trent, there appeared a phenomenon which P. Doyere describes thus: "The cenobite all too often regards the hermit as a freak, and tends to throw him out of the religious state. In the West, this has been the attitude of the ecclesiastical hierarchy which leans toward the cenobitic discipline and organization to the point of taking it as the very principle of the religious state."[11] To cover this period the Congregation of St Maur may serve as the example. In the *Life of the Just,* and the *History of the Congregation,* the only information we are given concerns superiors; nothing at all is said of simple monks. Lay brothers and oblates are barely mentioned. It is difficult to form any assessment on the common position regarding hermits. In "The Life of the Just," the only two requests for this form of life are made by superiors and are refused.[12] Nevertheless, in most of the accounts given here, two qualities are brought into relief: the desire to avoid the office of superior, and the yearning for the solitude of the cell, for silence, for austerity and for prayer.

Thus the Congregation had a very noble and very definite concept of monastic values. From the seventeenth century at least, these were strongly safeguarded, but at the same time the Congregation was heavily involved in political and cultural affairs. The office of superior involved continual contact with the world. As the superiors seem to have had high monastic ideals, one can readily appreciate their efforts to avoid the responsibility of office by being sent to provincial monasteries or even being able to live as hermits. But because the Congregation was highly centralized, the individual's interests were often sacrificed to those of the institution. This is clear from the reasons given for nominations to office. One could not say that the climate was unfavorable to the eremitical life.[13] But the interests and prestige of the Congregation could not adapt to the eremitical aspirations of men capable of furthering the common good. The scholarly commentators on the

11. P. Doyere, *art. cit.,* col., 980.

12. Martene, *Vie des justes* (3 ed., Heurtebize Liguge-Paris, 1926), pp. 20 et 139. *Histoire de la Congrégation de Saint Maur,* ed. G. Charvin (Liguge-Paris, 1930), 4:215.

13. We read in the Constitutions (ed. 1646): "The Superior General will permit those to whom and when he shall judge it expedient, to withdraw to cells prepared for this purpose, where, for a definite time they may be free from all mundane occupations and devote themselves wholly to things divine . . ."-quoted by P. Salmon in *Rev. d'hist. de l'Egl. de France* 43 (1957): 119, no. 60.

Rule, Dom Martene and Dom Mege, consider hermits from a purely historical viewpoint, not as a current problem.

Finally, during the last twenty years, the question of the eremetical life has gradually come to the fore again. The eremitic way, at first suspect, has been slowly accepted. Many monasteries now have hermitages and hermits attached to them. Here indeed is an example of that form of renewal which seeks to keep in line with tradition and to find in tradition the authentic meaning of monastic life. Another indication is in the special number of *Lettre de Ligugé* (Jan.-Feb., 1967) on the topic of the "Relevance of Eremitism." In the same year the review, *Vita Religiosa,* published by the Congregation of Religious, devoted two articles to the eremitical life. The problem of the relationship between the eremitic and cenobitic life involves structures as well as ideas.

In the West as in the East, the overall impression is that there is no theoretical basis for the eremitical life—that is to say, no general accepted "theory" deriving from tradition. There are theories—in the plural—however, and they are less rigid and absolute than one would have thought. But above all there are the facts of eremitism; there are personal vocations to be fulfilled in diverse ways. There is the one call, the monastic search for God. For most it is a call to community life.[14] The structure must be adapted to the facts. It will be minimal and sufficiently flexible to respect a plurality of graces. Tradition points us to a theological and practical consideration of charisms rather than giving us a doctrine or legislation on the relationship between the eremitic and cenobitic life. It seems best to consider in the light of tradition, then, the minimal structure to be created or restored for the furtherance of vocations.

TOWARD A STATUTE FOR HERMIT MONKS

In face of the renewal of the eremitic vocation, one can readily understand that ecclesiastical and monastic authori-

---

14. It is always with profit that one may re-read the carefully nuanced pages of P. Doyere, "Complexité de l'eremitisme" in *La vie spirituelle* 87 (1952): 243-254, in particular his conclusions on "Le cenobitisme et les vocations cremitiques."

ties are concerned about a statute for hermits. These do in fact exist, though Canon Law makes no provision for them. Such a statute should be based on tradition and should respect the values which tradition has preserved. On this matter two opinions have recently been expressed.

The first is that of Father Jacques Winandy. In 1959 he showed that Canon Law and the general attitude being what they are, the better thing would be for hermit monks to receive exclaustration. He emphasized the advantages of this, but also saw the disadvantages of exclaustration "at the bidding of the Holy See." With this it would seem that "the regular superiors of the one concerned would have no power to recall him to his monastery without the consent of the Holy See." "But" he added "one would wish for the creation of a new form of exclaustration for such cases, one which would be full adapted to the eremitical ideal and should be expressly related to a formal approbation of the eremitical life as a state of perfection."[15]

Two years later, in 1961, Father P. Doyere expressed the contrary opinion. For him "the legislation on enclosure provides the most effective context for an elaboration of a statute for hermit monks." The hermit monks connection with his religious family could easily be retained by adding a section to Canon 606 and by introducing a parallel measure in particular monastic constitutions; but he did not pretend that the problem was primarily canonical. "The main problem is the abbot." Father Doyere considered that an abbot concerned with the particular working of the Spirit in each soul should be able to recognize an eremitical vocation and allow its being followed outside the monastery, but it would be important to maintain a spiritual dialogue between the monk and abbot, *per se vel per alium.*[16]

Indeed, the hermit's dependence on his abbot extolled by Father Doyere accords fully with tradition. Ideally it is also

15. "Pour un statut canonique des ermites" in *Supplément de la vie spirituelle* 12 (1959): 343-351.

16. "Sur le statut des ermites monastiques. II: Perspectives actuelles" in *Supplement de la vie spirituelle* 14 (1961): 394-403.

the better solution. It is important, however, that such dependence be not purely juridical, lest the abbot soon tire of it and demand the hermit's exclaustration, or else his return to the community. A sustained spiritual dialogue would presuppose that the abbot in question and his successor would truly fill the role of spiritual fathers.

Where this condition is not present, there will be the temptation to supply for it with juridical stipulations. These could attempt to establish essential conditions—for example that the candidate for the eremitical life should have at least a certain age and a certain length of time as a professed monk. Precautions like this, under the guise of prudence, reveal only an incapacity to take any risk in the Holy Spirit. As for requiring that the candidate be "a perfect cenobite" of irreproachable life, this would introduce an element difficult to assess. As Father Doyere has written, the abbot "must not expect a prospective hermit to be perfect in every point before consenting to his request." The eremitic state is not a reward for merit but a way of perfection; those who embark on it are not required to be without faults, or motivated by absolutely pure intentions." Finally, tradition does not require necessarily a great length of time in community as probation.[17]

As Father Doyere indicates, tradition and monastic thought give the impression that it is best to set ones course in this direction by "unobtrusive experiments." But this presupposes an attempt to restore a sound mental approach and foster a spiritual climate, wherein all, the abbot and other cenobites, may grasp the value of the eremitical vocation for some. A

17. The Council in Trullo of 692 promulgated "Rules which obliged aspirants to the anachoretic life to live for three years in a monastery, followed by one year outside the enclosure by way of experience before their definitive retirement into the desert." See P. Canivet: "Erreurs de spiritualité et troubles psychiques" in *Recherches de sciences religieuses* 50 (1962): 175, with bibliography. These are some who are of the opinion that the *diuturna probitas* prescribed by the Rule of St Benedict (ch. 1:4) as a preparation for the life of a solitary, is not, according to the context, the terminology and the sources, any longer than the *morosa deliberatio,* which according to the same Rule (ch. 58:16) precedes the "vows" of the cenobite—which consists of a year. It will rest with philologists to decide this.

complete psychological and spiritual change is needed here analogous to what is under way in the field of ecumenism. Moreover, as Father Doyere states, a simplified observance might be in itself a form of eremitism, and suppress for some the nostalgia for the pure eremitic life. Finally the discernment of the vocation should not necessarily or exclusively fall on the abbot. It could involve the advice of a spiritual father whether he be a member of a monastic community or not. The abbot would avail himself of this advice before giving his own consent. Once he is allowed to live in the vicinity of the monastery, the hermit's security in his vocation should be safeguarded in regard to the two following points.

1. He should have the guarantee that he would only be recalled to the community in absolute necessity, and will have the right of appeal to a higher superior where there is disagreement. The main concern should be reverence for a vocation. It is important that the hermit's stability in his own vocation be assured.

2. The hermit should enjoy a certain autonomy. His rule should be approved by the abbot, but without the need to have recourse to the latter for frequent permissions.

Finally, whatever be the value of this suggestion, it should be possible to establish colonies, where hermits, temporary or otherwise, could more easily find a life-style adapted to their needs.[18]

18. An article on the colony of Hermits of St John Baptist in British Columbia, Canada, "The Hermits of Vancouver" in *Catholic Digest* (March, 1967), pp. 188-193, bears this sub-title: "They serve God and their fellowmen in the solitude of a desert on the Pacific Coast."

CHAPTER V

CONTEMPLATION AND THE CONTEMPLATIVE LIFE YESTERDAY AND TODAY[1]

VATICAN II IS SURPRISINGLY CONSISTENT in its use of the word "contemplation." Its first text, the *Constitution on the Sacred Liturgy*, uses the word "contemplation" twice in its introduction to characterize the true nature of the Church and indicate the goal of all her activity.[2] In chapter five of *Dogmatic Constitution on the Church*[3] it is used with reference to priests, and again in the *Decree on Priestly Life and Ministry*.[4] The document in which this terminology is most frequently met is one of the last, and the one in which it might be least expected, the *Pastoral Constitution on the Church in the Modern World*.[5] Here it is used four times, though sometimes in the broad sense. We find its specific meaning for Christianity in a second chapter of the *Constitution on Divine Revelation, Dei Verbum*,[6] where its significance is given a doctrinal development.

There the objective basis of all Christian contemplation is clearly presented. The Council recalls all that God did to reveal himself to mankind from the preparation of the Old Testament right through to his full revelation of himself in Jesus Christ. The Gospel accepted in faith by the apostles is handed on to us by Scripture and Tradition. The Constitution

1. *Vie consacrée* 40 (1968): 193-226.
2. No. 2.
3. No. 41.
4. No. 13.
5. Nos. 8, 56, 57, 59.
6. Nos. 7-8.

then indicates how Sacred Scripture and Tradition are like a mirror in which the pilgrim Church on earth sees God from whom she has received everything, until in the end she is brought to see him as he is, face to face.[7] Contemplation is, then, the work of the whole Church. It is her action or better, her response which is realized in her members in different ways, according to each one's gifts. The text makes this very clear a little further on, showing that our task is not the preservation of a static deposit but the promotion of development and growth, absorbing truth into our life. In the packed phrases of this document every word is important.

> This tradition, which comes from the apostles, develops (*proficit*) in the Church with the help of the Holy Spirit. For our understanding of the words and event handed down increases (*crescit*), and this in several ways: through the contemplation and reflection (*ex contemplatione et studio*) of believers treasuring all these things in the heart; through intimate understanding of their spiritual experience (*intima spiritualium rerum quam experiuntur intelligentia*) and through the preaching (*ex praeconio*) of those who have received the sure gift of truth through episcopal succession. For as the centuries succeed one another, the Church moves constantly forward toward the fullness of divine truth, until the words of God reach their complete fulfillment in her.[8]

Here we have fresh evidence of the eschatological tension shown by many of the Council texts;[9] it is not a matter of waiting for some teacher at the end of time; the mystery has already been communicated, received and possessed, in the ever present "now" of the Church's life, but this communication and possession are active, dynamic and continuous.

> The words of the holy fathers witness to the living presence (*vivificam praesentiam*) of this Tradition whose wealth is poured into (*transfunduntur*) the practice and life of the

7. No. 7.
8. No. 8.
9. Under the title "La vie contemplative et le monachisme d'après le concile Vatican II" in *Gregorianum* 47 (1966): 513-516, I have pointed out the texts.

believing and praying Church. Through the same Tradition the Church's full canon of Sacred Books is known (*inno-tescit*), and the Sacred Writings themselves are more profoundly understood (*penitus intelliguntur*), and unceasingly made active (*et indesinenter actuosae redduntur*) in her; and thus God, who spoke of old (*olim locutus est*), unceasingly converses (*sine intermissione . . . colloquitur*) with the bride of his beloved Son; and the Holy Spirit, through whom the living voice of the Gospel resounds in the Church and through her in the world, leads (*inducit*) unto all truth those who believe, and makes the word of Christ dwell abundantly in them.[10]

Much could be said about this text and its wonderful wealth of biblical references, but our point is to show its recognition of the fact that the activity of contemplation is one of the means by which the Church grows, advancing to her goal, and responding to the salvific intervention of her God revealing himself. In Scripture and Tradition, she sees him as in a mirror, and the colloquy, the intimate dialogue she holds with him is never interrupted. At root then Christian contemplation is not a psychological activity of the individual reaching out to God: mediation is needed. There is no contemplation without Scripture and the Church.

TRADITION

It will be remembered that the Council refers to the "teaching of the holy Fathers." It is really quite easy to trace the ideas and even the wording of these passages from *Dei Verbum* to the early writers on contemplative prayer. For they have often compared Scripture to a mirror,[11] they have often referred to the link between understanding and experience,[12] and shown how sacred history penetrates the mind through meditation, and gives us food for thought continually for daily

10. No. 8.
11. Texts are quoted in H. de Lubac, *Exégèse Médiévale*, 4 vols. (Paris, 1959), 1: 569.
12. *Ibid.*, pp. 569-570.

living.[13] They use the words "growth" and "progress,"[14] and speak of "deeper" or "loftier" penetration into the mysteries of salvation. Moreover, their treatment of contemplation is characterised by humility. As we gain a deep understanding and grasp of its bearing in our lives, our pride and arrogance will diminish. When we realize what we lack, how much is still needed for full, clear truth, we are grieved by this lack and we long to remedy it.[15] We experience in ourselves, according to the Psalm, what the Lord God has to say within us.[16]

The Council refers to a whole line of Tradition. To illustrate this we here give two quotations from Cassian, as one of the most influential writers in this field. At the beginning of the first quotation, we find expressions quite similar to those used in *Dei Verbum: crecente . . . cum proficiente, proficiet, studium, intelligentia.*"

> "In proportion as we renew our spirit by study, the face of Scripture is renewed and the beauty of holy understanding increases with our own progress. . . ."[17]

In another place he speaks of the "one who continues to progress" and who "is satiated with the most sublime and most mysterious teachings of the prophets and apostles" and gives us a well-known and wonderful passage (Here again we have the words *experimentia, meditatio* and *speculum* showing through the translation.):

> Drawing life from this food which he is constantly taking, he is so penetrated with the sentiments expressed in the psalms that he recites them, not as compositions of the Prophet, but as his own. And his whole approach is one of profound compunction. At the very least, he regards them as having been written especially for him and

13. *Ibid.,* pp. 558-568.

14. "Raising us to a more lofty perfection." Cassian, *Conferences,* 1:19; *Sources chrétiennes* 42:100.

15. "It is a matter of understanding increasing and pride decreasing . . . certain things are understood more thoroughly . . . sometimes he is caught up in more sublime contemplation and is sweetly tormented even to tears of desire for this joy."—St Gregory the Great, *In Ezek.* 22:2; PL 76:948.

16. Ps 84:9 (Vulgate) quoted by Cassian, *Conf.* 1; *Sources chrétiennes* 42:100.

17. *Conf.* 14:2; *Sources chrétiennes* 54:196.

knows that what they express was not realized once and for all in the Prophet, but is every day fulfilled in himself.

So it is that the Holy Scriptures reveal themselves to us more clearly, showing us their very heart and marrow. Our own experience helps us to understand them and we seem to know intuitively what they are expressing. The meaning of the words comes to us through our own experience, not through explanation. Our own reactions are those in which the Psalm has been sung or composed—and to that extent we are its authors. The Psalm expresses these dispositions, but we find in the mirror of our own experience the truth of what is expressed, and therefore understand more clearly. By letting our own reactions teach us, we find that they are less a subject to be learned than a reality to be experienced, and it is through experience that we understand them. Mere memorizing does not effect our understanding of the Psalms; they must be brought to birth in the depths of our heart as sentiments that are natural to us and part of our existence. Understanding comes from experience, not from reading.[18]

Such is the activity of Christian contemplation: it is contact with God through meditation on his word; it is wonder at his mysteries revealed in salvation history and consequently in the Church. Contemplation is lived with the Church and for her: she is God's salvation made present and operative in the world.

CONTEMPLATIVE LIFE

The meaning of contemplation sheds light on the meaning of contemplative life. This latter is mentioned in several Council documents in terms that leave no doubt as to its meaning: it is a state of life in which people give themselves to assiduous prayer and ready penance, in an atmosphere of recollection and solitude.[19] This last element implies some form of separation from the world. It may admit of degrees and must be well understood. In fact, as Paul VI explained in an address

18. *Conf.* 10:2; *Ibid.,* p. 92.
19. See "La vie contemplative . . . .," pp. 500-506.

on May 22, 1967, "the world" may mean either the whole of creation, the cosmos, as we say these days, or else humanity, as the theater of human drama, a meaning that comes through frequently in *Gaudium et Spes;* or finally, it may mean human nature as affected by sin, and this is the "world" of which St John and St Paul often speak.[20] It may also mean ordinary society, even Christian society, with the risk and the gain involved.

There are Christians who withdraw from the world in this last sense. While recognizing, esteeming, and admiring the values found there, they freely deny themselves certain of these in order to affirm others more clearly. Their baptismal renunciation leads them to break with the world of sin, to withdraw, retreat: in short, to use a term both biblical and tradition, to "go apart" into the solitude essential for purification and prayer. This voluntary withdrawal is actually a charism found in the Church from early times and still frequent today. Tradition gives it a double justification.

The first derives from the diversity of graces and vocations, from the variety of charisms. This is evident in Scripture, and Vatican II insists on it more than once: "the graces of the Spirit are different . . ."[21] and yet it is the same Spirit calling the faithful to live the same Christian life in different ways. Contemplatives have no right to withdraw from the world for any other motive than that which is common to all Christians; but they are asked to strive for it in a different way. On one hand, God is free, on the other, men are limited. It is quite legitimate then, for some to give themselves more intensely than others to this or that form of Christian response to the message of God. This is what is meant by "a limitation of spiritual consciousness—the fact that we cannot live out in depth a spiritual attitude without restricting the scope of our horizon and leaving complementary aspects aside! We cannot act on a this-worldly level without paying less attention

20. *Documentation catholique* 64 (1967), col 1169-1171.
21. *Gaudium et spes,* No. 38.

to God."[22] Nevertheless this "action" is as necessary and fruitful as the "attention." The *Constitution on Divine Revelation* enumerates various ways of contributing to the growth of the Word within the Church: *praeconium* is a specialization in proclaiming the message and produces different types of preachers; contemplation specializes in meditation on the same message and has given rise to the organization and development of the contemplative life, from the very early days of the church till now.

WITHDRAWAL IN SALVATION HISTORY

The Spirit is free to call some to this type of contemplative specialization and does so by another charism which provides further justification for the contemplative life: we refer here to the definitive role in salvation history of the eremitical way of life, as described in the preceding pages. The way of life lived by contemplatives is only a means by which they realize, according to a fixed plan, on the subjective level, the Christian challenge common to all the faithful. For those called to live the solitary life for God and with God this is the very condition of their sharing in salvation. It is also a preeminent way of contributing to their own salvation and to that of the whole world. Thus, it can be defined only in terms of its relationship with the salvific action of God, supremely free in Jesus Christ, and with the Word of God as efficaciously preserved in Scripture and Tradition. It is one of the forms assumed by the contemplation and consent given by the whole Church to Revelation, and one realizes that the interior understanding of the Bible and of the teaching of the Church play an important role here. In fact, they constitute the contemplative life, legitimise it and assure it of objective value and real efficacy. There is no authentic contemplative life without this inner penetration, and we have just shown how the Council even speaks of "experience" of the content of Holy Scripture. There is no contemplative life unless there is union with the whole Church and her hierarchy.

22. Ch. A. Bernard SJ, *La prière chrétienne* (Paris: Desclée de Brouwer, 1967), p. 12.

The saints and doctors who instituted and justified the contemplative life always based it on Scripture. Rather than any particular texts, it is a question of the broader pattern of religious events and the basic situations met in Scripture. These illustrate the role of withdrawal in salvation history.

The Old Covenant bears a very definite element of separation. Abraham is called to leave his family and country. Israel becomes a people by leaving Egypt, and even after passing through the Red See and the desert it is told to keep away from the Canaanites. The Exile both destroyed national structures and increased the people's consciousness of spiritual separation. Later, in the Hellenistic period, we have the Macchabees, the Pharisees and finally Qumran attaching increasing importance to this isolation from the pagan world.

The theme recurs in the New Testament. St Paul develops it with texts borrowed from Tradition: "Make no bond with infidels . . . what has the temple of God to do with idols? And we are the temple of the living God, for he himself said: 'I will dwell in the midst of you, and walk with you'; 'I will be their God and they will be my people'; 'Go out from the midst of these people and keep yourselves apart, says the Lord.' "[23]

But from this point on, the theme is radically transformed and every trace of the racial and legalistic element is left behind. The withdrawal is now "withdrawal from sin," and this for the purpose of intimacy and union with God. The Gospels show us the withdrawal and separation of St John the Baptist and then Jesus himself who went out to the desert to be tempted there, and on other occasions "went apart" for solitary prayer, and invited his disciples to do the same. This is the contemplative life of every Christian in the face of God and of himself, the foundation of any love of the world. Jesus preaches the Gospel of the Kingdom from his awareness that as Son, he knows the Father and possesses the Spirit. And so it is with every Christian, for in each one he lives by the Spirit. Every proclamation of God's message really continues Christ's proclamation of the good news of salvation, and all contemplative life is a sharing in the life of Jesus.

23. 2 Cor 6:14-17; cf. 1 Cor 5:13.

WITHDRAWAL IN THE DEVELOPMENT OF THE CHURCH

Tradition has interpreted these scriptural facts in two ways: by the fact of the contemplative life itself throughout the history of the Church, and by doctrine on the contemplative life, in the light of particular biblical themes.

The first thing clear from the facts is that this call to renounce the world has assumed many forms. The call is spiritual, historical, and incarnational, as we say these days. It is not to be bound up with any definite institutional form and yet it needs concrete expression. When the whole Church is a little flock spurned by the world, as in times of persecution, there is no reason at all for establishing communities to exemplify visibly her striving for purification and prayer in solitude. However, from early times there has been an asceticism stressing continence. When excessive, and when implying an opposition between spirit and matter, this tendency led to the Encratic heresy—Encratic meaning those who abstain. But within the Church herself, the tendency developed with more balance and regard for orthodoxy. Its strongest characteristic is a high esteem for virginity. Essentially, this is a form of separation from certain worldly values. There are analogous examples in the philosophy of the East, though exaggeration led to Manicheism. Greek philosophy too, especially Platonism, shows the same characteristics. Christian encratism leaves room for the human values expressed in these traditions. There are contingent elements in a synthesis like this; they have been legitimately accepted after careful sifting, but they are in need of further review today. It would be an undue simplification of the facts to explain them all in terms of their connection with this or that cultural trend, for they are really a proof of Christian humanism, the Church's capacity to assimilate human values. History provides repeated examples of this in every period—the Middle Ages, the Renaissance and especially the world of today.

From early times the Christians of the East, even more than those of the West, recognized the institutional forms of withdrawal as the sign of the ideal inspired by the Gospel and wit-

who have been, as it were, agents of the Spirit down through the ages.

Whatever its form, the contemplative vocation remains exceptional, and in this sense is extraordinary, in proportion to its endeavor to realize the mystery of salvation in a truly consistent way. The vocation is legitimate only when it fosters communion with the whole Church and contributes in its own way to her life. This necessity of universal communion presupposes that the contemplative should be free from any trace of egoism and purified from self-love to devote himself to universal love. This love is the basis of reciprocal responsibility between himself and the other members of the Church. Christians in the world have every right to seek help from those who have withdrawn from it. But these, in turn, are in no less need of the prayer of the others, if they are to be faithful to their difficult vocation.

THE CONTEMPLATIVE EXPERIENCE

What is the content of this contemplative life in our modern world? What occupation, or preoccupation should fill this leisure? None but the activity of contemplation spoken of by the Council, of which it is difficult to give any description beyond awkward and inadequate stammering. It is an obscure reality and is therefore difficult to analyze for it defies clarification. We must rest content with a broad, though honest description devoid of literary embellishment. The reality itself is both rich and simple: it means hearing the word of God. But if we are to be sure of hearing, we must listen, and eventually accept and act. This involves dialogue with God through meditation on his efficacious word. It involves the effort to penetrate to the depth of its meaning. In this sense we put ourselves to the test, integrating the word into our living. This will be our way of willing and fulfilling the plan of salvation, which is union between God and the whole human race, in Jesus Christ and in the Church. This will be our way of sharing in the dialogue of Christ with his Father through the Spirit. Basically, prayer is cooperation in the work of salvation accomplished in Jesus. In it we draw near to God, objectively and efficaciously, leaping over the gap that separates us from him, getting back to him and uniting ourselves wholly with him; this is what it means to be saved, to share in the salvation of all men. It is accomplished wholly through faith, though not without the collaboration of our faculties at works through them, beyond their ordinary and natural operation.

This habitual disposition of being present to God is essentially simple. That does not mean it is easy, but we should hold for sure that it is well within our reach. It is not an unrealistic or shadowy ideal. It lies within the ambit of the daily round and is exercized through the necessary activities of everyday life. Contemplative orders make some selection from all the activities open to Christians and retain only what is compatible with their preoccupation with God. There are priests, laymen and religious who are real contemplatives. Though not living the contemplative life, they devote themselves to the works proper to their own vocation, striving to permeate these with contemplation. But there are some who refuse to get involved in any kind of activity directly relating to the service of neighbor. They are few, and for them it is lawful. They are the exception. Others are willing to adopt some form of activity, so long as it remains the expression of their contemplation. It is not to be regarded as their goal but remains relative to it. This activity is not sought, but it is not refused; it remains subordinate to the primary commitment. This hierarchy of values is hard to maintain, since any sort of activity is absorbing, and makes less demand on a person than the contemplative experience.

It is essential to have a very clear notion, both sublime and realistic, of what the contemplative experience involves, if one is to prepare for it and persevere in it. It does not imply extraordinary psychic phenomena. It does not consist in great consolations of the sensitive order, or in violent mental strain. It is a humble, hidden and assiduous search. It involves waiting, devotion, intimacy, love, consent, reciprocal presence, wonder and admiration at God's work, solitude with him, silence, communion, sharing. It is God's plan actualized. It is

nessing to her life of faith. People have always placed great faith in the prayer and dedication of those who renounce other aims to follow this vocation. The word "contemplative" may be applied to it, for though originally platonic it has acquired a new, wider and fully Christian meaning. But this institution has always been the subject of renewal by the saints and by the Church's authority, for it is not the material observance, the letter, that unites to God, but the relentless spiritual search for him, which is part of the Church's own life.

And yet, the contemplative life has not always steered clear of abuses and deviations down through the centuries. There has always been the temptation of attaching to material separation, and similar observances, a salvific value in their own right. While some have fallen victim to this, the Church's reformers have always reacted against it, as against similar dangers. The position adopted at the Protestant Reformation was perhaps extreme. On this point it affirmed a kind of excessive, almost desperate, exasperation in adhering to a truth always maintained by the Catholic Church and seen today in a new light by the Churches even outside Catholicism: the doctrine that a certain type of union with God demands withdrawal and isolation essentially spiritual in nature, deriving from and exemplified by the New Testament. To this material separation must always be subordinate.

DOCTRINE

Such are the facts about this life of withdrawal within the Church. Its doctrine is set forth by the Fathers and by spiritual writers of all times including our own. They are quick to point out that the contemplative withdrawal is really a deeper and therefore "typical" realization of religious values, as shown by the persons and events in the Bible: the vocation of Abraham, the Exodus, the period of purification in the desert, the symbolic character of some of the prophets like Elijah, Elisha and the "sons of the prophets," Mount Carmel, the vision of Ezekiel. Later, we have St John the Baptist living a penitential life in the desert, while waiting to point out the one who was to come. Above all, there is Jesus. We know that he retired to a mountain, symbolic of solitude, "to be tempted there," to devote himself to prolonged prayer, to be transfigured in the glorious light of Thabor, to pass through his agony and death to the resurrection, and finally, to manifest his return to the Father. Of Mary, we know that she "listened to the word and meditated on it in her heart." The same pattern is shown by the community at Jerusalem, which gave itself to prayer.

There are other features of this life. We see from it that eschatological fulfillment is ever in process. Through faith, contemplation anticipates complete union with God—a union that is symbolized by the return to paradise, the sabbatical rest, the endless chant of the alleluia, by unshakable love, by union with the angels adoring and praising God and proclaiming his glory. This expresses the traditional idea of the "angelic life," and it has nothing in common with that false angelism that simulates an imitation of the angels, of whom we know so little. All these elements and aspects of salvation history are realized in a specific way by those called to the contemplative life. They hearken to the word, they hear and heed it. They unfold and live Christ's mysteries in their own lives, and therefore also in the Church. Through a life that is formed by the sacraments and by the Gospel, they strive for this intimate union with the Word, and find it symbolized for them in the *Song of Songs* and in the spiritual nuptials of virginal consecration to the Spouse. In every possible way they endeavor to live wholly under the influence of the Holy Spirit sent by the risen Jesus to his Church.

A constitutive bond with the Church is therefore essential to the contemplative life and it should be a bond in which all the aspects of salvation are realized in fidelity to the diverse gifts and vocations and therefore will be expressed in a variety of life-styles. There is room for different types of eremitical life and different types of common life. Some will give greater stress to one or other of the biblical and traditional themes recalled above. In fact, this is evident from the existing complementary traditions deriving from those founders and fathers

salvation being accomplished in a Christian and through him in the Church.

In a word, contemplation is encounter with the Father, in Jesus, through the Spirit. It is a response to the word of salvation spoken by him. The entire Church is drawn close to him through the grace which the contemplative receives personally. He experiences it in depth as a continuous and forceful challenge. Though possessing it in the certainty of faith, yet he yearns for it in the obscurity of that same faith. He remains in God's presence as one who needs and seeks him. While thanking God for the salvation he has received, he continues to beg for it. God has become a personal reality for him and reveals him to himself as the person he really is —both his nobility and his utter poverty. The experience of the contemplative is not necessarily (or often) exalting but rather healthfully humbling. It is an experience of poverty, of a radical difficulty in corresponding to the initiative by God. And yet it is not a depressing or discouraging experience: it is based on God's fidelity to his people, to his Church, to each one of those who believe in him. It is the trial of man's fidelity. It is his chance to hope, to pray and so, to obtain ever more. It is a context in which salvation is achieved.

St Bernard's monks confided their dryness, dispiritedness, dullness and stupidity of soul to him. He answered with strong words their laments of being "incapable of understanding deep and learned realities about God" and "experiencing nothing or almost nothing of the Spirit's sweetness." Are they going to give up the quest? "They sigh, aspiring to receive the spirit of wisdom and understanding."[24] If they are to resist distraction in their search, he insists, they must resist being caught up in easier occupations. Only at this price will they be gradually purified. Not satisfied or content with themselves, they must simply be faithful on their side as God is faithful and because he is. They share his fidelity. It reassures and strengthens them.[25]

---

24. *Sup. Cantica* 9:3; *S. Bernardi opera*, 1:43-44; CF 4:55.

25. Recalling the experience of St Paul would help to a better understanding, by contrast, of the contemplative experience, with which the experience of the Apostle offers some points in common: See for example P. Fisch SJ, "Comme le Père m'a envoyé, moi aussi je vous envoie" in *Revue diocésaine de Tournai* 22 (1967): 421-434.

THE CONDITIONS OF PRAYER

If this humble and often humbling experience is to be followed up, then special conditions are essential: silence, recollection, austerity and prolonged attention to the salvific word of God. The contemplative experience is to be won not by introversion but by openness, especially by openness to God's work. The contemplative "lives in silence and the more intently he does so the more receptive he becomes to God's word, his ear ever attuned to it."[26] He does not seek delight, but only to offer himself. Sometimes he feels that God is forgetting him. But his dedication to God is beyond all feeling and subsists in faith. Even when he feels that he is attaining a better grasp of what he believes, he must unceasingly renew his surrender. New lights bring new problems. As his union with God becomes deeper, so too does his yearning. He is constantly torn between what he has and what he longs for, between what he already is and what he wants to become by gradual transformation from light to light, in the glory of the Lord. He knows that this glory will be his portion only after death. In the meantime, he surrenders entirely to grace, that is, to the generosity and bounty of God. By the gift he receives from God he shares in the experience of faith in God and fidelity to him—like that of the prophets, the apostles, Mary, the saints and all the faithful, each one having a greater or lesser share through their human existence in the total experience of God which was, and is, Jesus' experience.

Everything in the contemplative life must be directed toward this humble experience of God. Everything must be subordinated to it and judged by the extent to which it fosters it. We do not mean an accumulation of observances, even of prayer. The institution must serve the goal of the person. No longer do we hold fast to the practices of former times. They had their value then, but this is not enough justification for keeping them now. There should be some development parallel with the apostolate. At present, everything connected with preaching the word of God is being revised. We have new methods and new techniques. The apostolate is not identical with the method and is ever outstripping it. So, too, must

26. J. M. Burocoa, *Tours de cloître* (La Pierre-qui-Vire, 1967), p. 2.

it be with the contemplative life. It must profit by the advances made in biblical, liturgical and patristic studies, in contemporary thought and in the psychological and sociological sciences. The modern conscience does not develop, react or communicate in the same way as formerly. Modalities that matched the aesthetic norm of yesterday are not necessarily agreeable to modern ears or modern taste. They do not necessarily fit in with the modern potential or meet current needs. Moreover, different countries, different types of civilization will express themselves in different ways. Contemplatives are not called by the Spirit to preserve in the Church vestiges of the past.

FORMS OF PRAYER

Hesitant though they may be, modern contemplatives like their early and medieval predecessors have a real duty since Vatican II to discover forms of prayer that will foster the prayer-experience of the whole Church, as comprehended in their personal vocation. These forms should not be copied from Christians leading a different type of life, nor should they be borrowed from the past, even the recent past. Their common prayer will not be the occasion of renewed spiritual stimuli, though these may benefit some, at a certain age, provided they are not too frequent. Nor will it be that sort of spiritual sweetness which might occupy them, while they remain in God's presence, but would leave them more passive, less personally involved than most modern people want to be. Still less will it be a strictly juridical obligation, with all the details settled in advance and deriving importance from that very fact.

Recent work on the history of the Eucharist and the Office has drawn renewed attention to the place formerly given to recollection and listening to the word of God.[27] It is not suf-

27. Cf. L. Bouyer. *Eucharistie. Théologie et spiritualité de la prière eucharistique* (Tournai, 1966), in particular the first chapters and the conclusions, pp. 429-440, and A. de Vogüé, "Le sens de l'office divin d'après la Règle de S. Benoît." in *Revue d'ascét. et de myst.* 42 (1966): 389-404; 43 (1967): 21-33.

ficient to say many words, even though they might be taken from Scripture or spiritual books. Rabelais had strong criticism for those who "mumble great slabs of reading and psalmody that they do not even understand, and say a lot of Our Fathers, interspersed with Hail Marys, without reflection or comprehension." He added "I call this mockery, not prayer." In place of this type of prayer-production the Catholic sense of Rabelais suggested another form of piety that has, in fact, always been followed by contemplatives. "All true Christians of every state, place and period pray to God. The Spirit prays and intercedes for them, enabling them to please God."[28]

It is not a matter of the length of time spent in "formal prayer," as some call it, but of the manner in which such time is spent, or as others would say, "the experience that fills it." "The exercise of prayer is useless if prayer of the heart does not inform one's whole life. Is a long period spent calmly before God, in conventual observance, in silence or in the recitation of many Psalms an adequate expression of purely personal prayer? Let us understand the aspiration, which so many contemplatives are now voicing, for a less liturgical prayer and life, in the recent sense of the word "liturgical." What these contemplatives want is a less formal prayer expressed in new forms better adapted to their inmost needs. It is not denied that the liturgy is prayer! But the need is felt for a more prayerful liturgy. People do not want it to be an external function carried out according to certain laws, decrees and rubrics and conformed to a refined aesthetic sense—but rather, a means of going to God and of personal encounter with him. Less texts, less words, less ceremonies: more silence, genuine recollection, interior dialogue. More continuity between the basic activity of all Christian contemplation, which is a listening to the word of God in reading, whether private or common, and the conventual expression of this prayer in worship. It is encouraging to learn that there are many communities where the reform of the liturgy, under

28. _Gargantua_, 1, 40, quoted by J. Krailsheimer, _Rabelais, Les écrivains devant Dieu_ (Paris: Desclée de Brouwer, 1967), p. 107.

the watchful eye of the Church, is heading in this direction. The Holy Spirit who calls Christians to contemplative experience helps their weakness. He helps them find a way of keeping alive this "Abba, Father" which sums up the whole prayer of Jesus in his members.

THE ECCLESIAL VALUE OF THE CONTEMPLATIVE LIFE

From early times, the life of separation from the world for prayer and asceticism has gone hand-in-hand with the growth of the Church through evangelization. This is a fact of history: *contemplatio* has always accompanied *praeconium*. We could prove the truth of this by borrowing examples from the Early Middle Ages. For instance, a bishop asked St Pachomius to make a foundation near him to help in his own way to overcome the resistance to truth.[29] St Boniface wanted missionary activity to be completed by that of the contemplatives.[30] And in our own times, Vatican II has declared that contemplative houses are essential in all churches,[31] the new as well as the old. It has dispensed those who live the purely contemplative life from all direct participation in the "various pastoral ministries" and this "in spite of the urgent needs of souls and the lack of diocesan clergy."[32] This courageous stand is equivalent to a doctrinal statement of greatest importance: the presence in the Church of Christian men and women devoted exclusively to the contemplative life is so necessary that it outweighs all other considerations, even the most urgent.

What is the reason for this? Because this life, like the apostolate, contributes to the progress of the Church, increases the efficacy of God's word within her, and assures her continuance of salvation history. Like the apostolate, the contemplative life exacts, contains and fosters an act of faith which is a participation of Jesus' contemplation of the Father

29. L. Th. Lefort, *Les vies coptes de S. Pachôme* (Louvain, 1943), p. 248.
30. In *Témoins de la spiritualité occidentale* (Paris, 1965), pp. 36-38, I have quoted the texts.
31. *Decree on Missionary Activity in the Church,* 18 and 40.
32. *Decree on the Pastoral Duty of Bishops,* 35.

through the Spirit. In both cases, it is the radiance of God's light and the fertility of his grace. This is realized first of all in the particular Church—that of the city, region, diocese or country—in which the contemplatives live out the exigencies of their vocation.[33] They must enter into the needs of this particular Church and take its pastoral needs into account. Therefore, their forms of organization and their observances will differ with different types of civilization, according to the judgment of the communities themselves and the local hierarchy.

But the tradition has always recognized a universal apostolic efficacy for the contemplative life. It has a role of fruitfulness for the whole Church. As this life is a means of tending to perfect charity, it supposes and fosters zeal for souls, and is a means of intercession and satisfaction for all. Again, it has always been admitted that there are cases when the contemplative, responding to the call of God and the Church, should speak to the world or even return to it for the sake of witness, either by example or by the spoken or written word.

These facts bring up some fine points for reflection, and the current advance in theology paves the way for their solution. Has the time come for resolving the dilemma so well formulated by Father Bouyer, between "a Christianity absolutely theocentric and contemplative: a Christianity which never for a single moment yields to the temptation to see in God merely a source of energy to be exploited for the good of humanity," and on the other hand "a Christianity in which the love that we have for God demands that we make other people love him?"[34] Before we attempt to reconcile these two apparently divergent tendencies, we might recall that, over the course of centuries this combination has assumed various forms and received varied motivations. It may be well not to claim that we have found a perfect synthesis today or reached a final solution. For we are dealing with the mystery of salvation, and even the Church's realization of this mystery is still growing.

33. *Ibid.,* 28.
34. *The Cistercian Heritage,* tr. E. Livingston (Westminster, Maryland: Newman, 1958), p. 202.

WHAT HISTORY HAS TO SAY

The strong sense of solidarity between the Church as a whole and those who have withdrawn from the world for a life of prayer has been more or less conscious and explicit at different periods. It is very keen at the present time—keener perhaps than ever before—and this is cause for real joy. Still, this is nothing new. A few examples will recall the attitudes of previous periods.

In early times, Origen proposed that Christians and especially ascetics should be exempt from compulsory military service because they personify all the conditions of military training by their life-long spiritual battle with the devils. These devils are the instigators of war, so that the saints are the vanguard in battle against them, for they strike at the root of the evil.[35] The man who fights to overcome the evil in himself is doing so in the name of all and on behalf of all. Together with them and for their good, he shares in the passion of Christ. Hence the collective efficacy of what Origen called "martyr-dom of conscience:" the more Christians there are to labor at their own sanctification, the less is evil free to act in the world. By robbing the serpent of his venom we keep him from injuring others.[36] This applies not only to victory over heresy but over every form of scandal and sin.

Later on, it was said that the world was really living on the merits of its solitaries.[37] A bishop, St John Chrysostom, spoke in praise of solidarity, concord and friendship as the source of charity, and added "But what about those who live in the mountains?" He was referring to the desert solitaries. "Well, they are certainly not short of friends. Quite the contrary. You will not find these solitaries in the market-place but they really have many friends who are united to them in the bond of charity. This is the whole purpose of their withdrawal and enables them to pray more than ever for the whole world. It is the highest form of friendship."[38]

35. Texts are quoted by S. Tavares Bettencourt-*Doctrina Ascetica Origenis* (Vatican, 1945), pp. 54 and 85.
36. *Ibid.,* pp. 120-123.
37. Pseudo-Rufinus, *Lives of the Fathers,* 3, Prol; PL 73:739.
38. *In Joan hom.* 78:4; PG 59:426.

Somewhere else, this same Father writes: "The strongest characteristic of the faithful lover of Christ is his spirit of service to his brothers, and his concern for their salvation. There are also the monks, living in the mountains and crucified in every possible way to the world. And again, there are those here present, listening to me. May one and all, in their own measure, come to the help of those in charge of the Churches, strengthening them with prayer, union of heart and charity. All should realize that their help is needed in every possible way and that distance is no factor. Those whom God's grace has chosen for ecclesiastical office and burdened with great responsibility need support in prayer. Otherwise their life will lack value and their talent will be so much empty wisdom."[39]

The Emperor Justinian echoes this same tradition: "The solitary life filled with contemplation is a reality in the order of holiness. It raises souls to God and helps everyone, even those who do not live it, through the purity that it demands and the prayer that is its substance."[40] Again, Theodore the Studite speaks of "the man who has time only for God, yearning for and preoccupied with God only. His one desire is to serve God alone, and in his peace with God he becomes a source of peace for others."[41] Finally, we give one more witness to the tenth-century tradition in the East. One writer says of the contemplative: "He is like God. His tenderness and charity are completely disinterested. He listens to everything and everyone, following God's own universal love and tenderness, looking for no return. He gives himself to God as a voluntary sacrifice of reparation. In Christ's humility, he accepts every kind of suffering on behalf of all, for his love embraces all. In his love for God he suffers and supports everything. Because of his universal love he is undaunted even by the trial of death by fire."[42]

39. *Contra Anomaeos* 6:3; PG 48:752, following the translation of J. M. Leroux, "Monachisme et communauté chrétienne d'après S. Jean Chrysostome" in *Théologie de la Vie Monastique* (Paris, 1961), p. 171, quoted by P. Deseille, *"L'Évangile au désert"* (Paris, 1965), p. 43.

40. *Novellae* 133, Pref. ed. Schoell-Kroll, *Corpus Iuris Civilis* (Berlin, 1912), 3:666, quoted as an insert in *Millénaire du Mont-Athos* (Chevetogne, 1963) 1:12.

41. *Petites catéchèses* 39 ed. Auvray, pp. 142-143, quoted in *L'Evangile au désert*, p. 104.

42. Ed. J. B. Chabot, "Vie du Moine Raban Youssef Bousnaya" in *Revue de l'Orient chrétien* 3 (1898): 79.

In both East and West, during the Middle Ages, those who withdrew from men did not cease to be involved with them as brothers. This was expressed by intercessory prayer, by the forms of dedication just mentioned and by works of charity for all in their spiritual and material needs. Recently, a historian asked what one could expect to find in any of the great monasteries of the eleventh century. He was referring to England, and replied to his own question: "For the people of that period, the monastery expressed the sum total of religious ideals, the needs of a whole society. . . ." When laymen founded monasteries they were setting up centers for prayers and intercession, fulfilling a service required by the ideal of the founders and the good of society in general.[43] It was not a matter of establishing centers for private exercises. An American of our own times reminds us of the extent to which monks of the past were an integral part of their own contemporary life by the following example: "The Cistercians of northern England in the twelfth century played a role analogous to that of General Motors in the United States today. The wool from Cistercian barns was one of the most important factors in England's economy during the middle ages."[44]

This could lead us on to many examples of contemplatives who were aware of their responsibility towards others. For instance, St Mauguille the hermit. He lived alone in complete isolation, applying himself to psalmody, watching and to interior prayer. By compunction he strove to expiate the widespread evils of the world as if they were his own sins. His genuine desire was that all should be saved and come to the truth.[45] There was yet another who prayed that all people should receive pardon and forgiveness for their sins.[46]

Among those who lived the common life, at Cluny, for example, we are told that St Mayeul's life was "one of adoration toward God and love of his goodness. Through the practice of daily mortification he became a victim pleasing to God

43. W. Urry, *Canterbury under the Angevin Kings* (London, 1967), p. 155.
44. T. Merton, "Openness and Cloister" in *Cistercian Studies* 2 (1967): 316.
45. *Vita Maldegesili;* PL 74:1444-1445.
46. *Vita S. Victoris; Acta SS. Boll,* Feb. 3:671.

on the altar of heavenly contemplation, by which he obtained what might have been thought impossible, both for his own salvation and that of others."[47] Again, Peter the Venerable, one of his successors, declared that "Although monks do not administer the sacraments, they contribute greatly to the salvation of the faithful."[48] One of the early Carthusians expressed similar convictions.[49] We have nuns like St Hildegarde[50] and many other witnesses from the medieval period. Intercession and intervention on behalf of others were not a motive, let alone *the* motive of their vocation. Yet, before God, this concern weighed heavily on their soul. They did not consider their life as one for the salvation of others, but as one in which the salvation of others had a necessary place. Their goal was union with God and this union resulted in union with all men: to live for God, and yet to live in union with all. Or, as someone has expressed it, "to live in the plural."

The early Cistercians, real *periti* of charity, have given doctrinal expression to this way of life. Two passages from Isaac of Stella will exemplify this:

> Any form of life is pleasing to God if it honestly expresses our love toward God and toward our neighbor for God's sake. Habit and observances are immaterial. It is for charity that things must be done or not done, changed or left unchanged. Charity is the sole principle on which we must act, the goal toward which we must aim. There can be no fault in what is in all truth done for charity and according to its spirit. Without charity nothing can be done. . . .[51]

> So brethren, let us make charity our norm of life, for it is the rule of sanctity. To live with Christ, in thought and desire in this heavenly fatherland, and yet to refuse no opportunity of charity for Christ through the long course of our laborious pilgrimage. To follow Christ on his way to the Father, to improve, simplify and unify oneself in quiet

47. *Vita brevior* 26 in *Bibliotheca Cluniancensis* (Paris, 1654), p. 1779.
48. *Epist.* 1:28; PL 189:142; ed. G. Constable (Cambridge, Mass., 1967), p. 82.
49. Guigo the Ancient, *Consuetudines* 20:2; PL 153:675.
50. *Scivias* 2:5; PL 197:488, translated in J. Leclercq, *The Life of Perfection*, tr. L. Doyle (Collegeville: Liturgical Press, 1961), p. 41.
51. Sermon 31; PL 194: 1792-1793.

meditation, to follow Christ in our encounter with our brother, to exert oneself in action, to share oneself in a thousand small things. To become all things to all men, to underestimate nothing that touches Christ, to thirst for only one thing and to be concerned with only one thing when it is a question of the one Christ, to desire to serve all men when it is question of the whole Christ.[52]

At a later period, the intention to contribute efficaciously to the salvation of others is still more explicit. The sixteenth-century Carthusian Lanspergius wrote: "Some withdraw completely from the company of men in order to be of greater service to those whom they leave. This withdrawal frees them for their purpose of living for their own and their neighbor's greater good."[53] Soon after this, St Teresa of Avila expresses the idea of combat for God. Hers is similar to the thought of Origen, which we have seen: Carmels are the bastions of prayer in the outposts of the Church.[54] Their religious must serve souls by meriting for them and by doing penance to prevent souls from being deprived of God's glory.[55] They speak to God on behalf of men, and share in the work of Jesus who was crucified even though he was God.[56] This provides us with a psychological dimension for the mystery of presence to men by nearness to God, a presence for which the whole of tradition vouches. Finally, quite near our own times we have Claudel's suggestion for the foundation of a Carmel in one of the Asian countries. Someone asked him how he could want a Carmel in a place where there were no Christians. "How can you expect to have Christians," he replied, "if there is no Carmel?"

AWARENESS OF BEING MEMBERS

If we try to discover the common element in these successive and diverse manifestations of the solidarity of contempla-

---

52. Sermon 12; PL 194:1730-1731.

53. *De vera religione et monasteriis* 15 in *Opera omnia* (Montreuil, 1910) 4:19.

54. *Way of Perfection,* cc. 1 and 3; tr. A. Alexander (Westminster, Maryland: Newman, 1953), pp. 1ff and 12ff.

55. *Life Written by Herself,* ch. 32; tr. D. Lewis (London: Baker, 1924), pp. 298ff.

56. "Interior Castle," Fourth Mansion, c. 3 in *St Teresa's Complete Works,* tr. E. A. Peers (New York: Sheed and Ward, 1963), 2:258ff.

tives with the Church, we should probably reach a conclusion something like this: they are fully aware of being members of the Body of Christ, and consequently, fully aware of living, praying, struggling, sanctifying and sacrificing themselves in union with the entire body and on its behalf, even when not expressly thinking of this. For when they forget men to think of God, they are still serving them. Just as Christ is "with the Father" before he is "for men" and "with men."[57] So too, in Christ, does the contemplative will to be continually with the members of Christ, with all who receive from the Father and in the Spirit the grace of the salvation won by Christ. The contemplative is associated with the whole Church in its sharing in the word of God, and the whole Church shares the benefits, the grace, which the contemplative receives both for himself and for all.

It may be good to say a word here about "vicarious substitution," by which the contemplative seems to give himself to God "on behalf of" the world and somehow in its stead. There is no ban on this kind of approach—in fact, it is the real main-spring for some contemplatives. But the contemplative vocation is primarily for God, in that God is its source and its goal. It is only in this context that the world has any place in the contemplative vocation. The current insistence that it is "for the world" is legitimate but secondary and wholly dependent on the full priority given to God and the orientation of one's life toward him. One gives oneself to him as part of the whole body, not as an individual offering himself in place of others, but as a member wanting to be a living member. The more he is a member of the body, the greater is his desire to be so, for his vocation is to foster the mystery of salvation by contemplation rather than by proclaiming it and yet in perfect communion with those who foster its growth in any other way.

As the call becomes more diversified and is, for some, a longing to attend on God alone,[58] the more universal is the solidarity that it engenders. Very early in the Bible there is a changeover from the responsibility of the clan to that of the

57. Cf. H. U. von Balthasar, "Relation immédiate avec Dieu" in *Concilium* 29 (1967): 39-53.
58. *Perfectae caritatis,* 7.

individual—in the matter of retribution, for example. At the beginning it was the whole community that suffered for the faults of one of its members or gained by one's fidelity; and the clan, the people of God as a whole, was considered to be just or sinful in comparison with other nations that did not know God.[59] But with Ezekiel and the parable of the sour grapes it becomes clear that God is concerned about each person; even in the heart of Israel there are sinners as well as just men. In the New Testament we have just men as well as sinners even outside of Israel. But the just are all united in a greater Israel, the universal Church, which is the true Israel. St Paul showed that it is a matter of indifference whether one is a Jew or a Gentile, and that we are all members of one another. This combination of personal with universal salvation reached its apex in Jesus Christ. It is primarily in himself that he has saved us; not by substitution but by a love that is contagious, warming, communicative and efficacious.

On this theme of contributing to the salvation of others, the early Rules evince a moderation that is sure proof of humility. There is no attempt to place on a candlestick or lofty pedestal the institute for which these early Rules were written. Not only St Antony but many of the Desert Fathers asked the same question "How shall I be saved?" The Jews who came to St John Baptist asked the same thing: "Master, what must we do?"[60] So did the rich young man: "Master, what must I do to have eternal life?"[61] And later, the first disciples who came to Peter and the apostles asked "Brethren, what must we do?"[62] Moreover, St Benedict's Prologue, which gives the basic interior approach of those who come to his school, requires no other motive than that of personal salvation.

"FOR MEN"

This first question and its reply have never excluded consideration for one's fellow men. The whole life of St Antony

---

59. See, e.g., A. Cause, *Du groupe ethnique à la communauté: Le problème sociologique de la religion d'Israël* (Paris, 1937).
60. Lk 3:12.
61. Mt 10:17.
62. Acts 12:37.

shows this. St Pachomius welcomed those who came to him
to work out their own salvation. And this has always been the
case. It is rare for solitaries to want to be completely alone or
to have no desire at all to share with others their own spiritual gifts for which they are so grateful to God. And yet, this
altruistic love, this longing for the salvation of all, was rooted
in their desire for personal union with God. When the Lord
suggested to Moses that he could be saved on his own, Moses
agreed only on condition that the whole of Israel should share
in this salvation. Loving God, he loved God's people also,
for God's sake. The same St Paul who declared "I desire to be
dissolved and to be with Christ"[63] also wanted to be anathema
for his brethren, and wrote "Woe to me if I do not preach the
Gospel."[64] Christ has involved all men in his own return to the
Father, but only through his resurrection.

Our solidarity is nothing new to God. He loves us only as
members of the human race. He is pleased with this saint, or
that, only for the same reason. When one member of the human
race gives him cause for joy, this redounds to the good of all.
He does not send his rain on just one lovely flower, but on
good and wicked alike. So the contemplative asking salvation
for himself alone in consciousness of his utter need of it wins
salvation for others as well. And when he prays for pardon
and grace he is only thinking of himself, because he knows his
own sinfulness. But in reality he is admitting the poverty of
all humanity in his own person. And all humanity gains by
his prayer, his desire and the gift given him in abundance. His
prayer is a service to his neighbor, though it need not necessarily be for his neighbor's intention. Prayer has a value of its
own, independently of its object or occasion. Its efficacy derives from the fact of being addressed to God. Someone has
said: "The big thing is to be conscious not so much of whom
one is praying for, but of whom one is praying to."[65] We think
that we are keeping our fervor up by the psychological tactic
of listing intentions, whereas it must derive primarily from our
conviction that the Lord is all powerful and worthy of adora-

63. Phil 1:23.
64. 1 Cor 9:16.
65. L. Bouyer, *The Meaning of Monastic Life* (New York, Kennedy, 1955), p. 144.

tion, that he is love and wants to be loved. To pray for various intentions, no matter how numerous these may be, is to limit the universal scope of prayer. God is the common Father of all men, and any prayer to him redounds to the profit of all men.

Those not living the contemplative life are much given to considerations about its usefulness to men. This is a legitimate approach but it hardly amounts to a reason for living such a life, or even to being the deciding factor in a vocation. "Nothing in the World is more intensely alive and active than purity and prayer," wrote Teilhard, "which hang like an unmoving light between the universe and God."[66] The contemplative may not think of placing himself between the world and God, but God sees him there. God recognizes and accepts his mediation. People often say that communities of prayer are lightning-conductors for a society that has forgotten God. Again, this may be how God sees them, but they themselves do not try to assume this attitude before him. They are lightning-conductors without trying to be. And they are perhaps more effective as lightning-conductors the less they try.

What is true in the dimension of prayer is also true in the dimension of witness, or of any other form of reality. Quite recently the Message of Contemplatives to the Synod of Bishops[67] has stressed this deep solidarity. It was shown that all the fecundity in a life like this—whether in prayer or in sacrifice—is rooted in a sharing in the sufferings and temptations which make it harder today than ever before to keep the faith in spite of its obscurity and to conform to it in actual living. The place of contemplatives in this struggle is silent and hidden, and yet, like others, as well as for and with others, they represent and actualize the mystery of Christ's temptation and triumph, death and resurrection.[68] There is no need, then, for all men or even all Christians to understand the nature of all vocations. There is no need for contemplatives to give an explanation of their vocation that will be under-

66. *Hymn of the Universe* (New York: Harper and Row, 1965), p. 154.
67. Text in *Documentation catholique* 64 (1967): 1907-1910.
68. Under the title "Chronique de l'actualité contemplative, I: Contemplation et athéisme" in *Novelle revue théologique* 100 (1968): 67-72, I have commented on this "Message."

stood by all. Père Loew writes: "The sign of the Absolute, of God, is 'to be,' rather than 'to be a sign.' It is not for some purpose that men understand the transcendence of God, but because it is a fact."[69] Father de Lubac writes: "Most Christians, nowadays at any rate, do not bother to ask whether their faith is up-to-date or efficacious. They are content to live in faith as the basic and increasingly relevant reality. They know the fruits deriving from it are good and profitable, even though hidden."[70] When any Christian intensifies his participation in the word of God and the mystery of salvation, all Christians gain by his intensified involvement, not just he. And when a contemplative deepens his life in God's presence and sees his own poverty and need as the grounds for greater humility, trust and gratitude for graces received, he becomes capable of sharing his experience with others, though he has not sought the experience nor been given it for that purpose. But his witness and his sharing will not distract him. They will prolong his experience and provide the occasion and the material for more intimate union with God. Perhaps it will not come his way to speak of it. Well and good, since the important thing, for himself and for others, is the fact of his experience and the deepening of the world's participation in the work of salvation.

From this we see how contemplatives can be said "to be obliged to cooperate in the salvation of the world, not by action or by intention but by their perfection. Not actively or deliberately but existentially."[71]

THREE CONTEMPLATIVE WITNESSES

Some profitable reflections are being expressed today about man as a "being-in relation," and about the communication, reciprocity and love which are part of his nature, just as they

69. "Le monastère, signe et témoinage" in *Collectanea Cisterciensia* 27 (1965): 166. In the same sense could be quoted A. Stolz, *L'ascèse chrétienne* (Chevetogne, 1948), p. 46; T. Merton, *Seeds of Contemplation* (New York, 1949), p. 158 and many other spiritual works of our days.

70. *New Paradoxes* (Paris, 1954), p. 95. The whole of this page, and the whole of its context are a warning against the tempation of immediate "efficacy."

71. I. Hausherr SJ, "La théologie du monachisme chez S. Jean Climaque" in *Théologie de la vie monastique* (Paris, 1961), p. 406.

are part of the nature of the God-man.[72] It seems hardly necessary then to develop our own considerations of that here. We offer only a brief survey on the question "What is the reason for the contemplative life?" We will conclude our thoughts not with more theory but with the example of the witness of three of those who have lived this life and helped to unravel the problem.

John XXIII said that Teresa of Avila was "convinced that prayer and the love of sacrifice are extremely important for the salvation of souls, and constitute an important form of the apostolate."[73] But this efficacy was not the reason for her entrance into Carmel.

St Thérèse of Lisieux wrote of herself: "Jesus awaits the prayer of a poor little soul to save other souls."[74] And again: "Jesus asks us to quench his thirst by giving him souls."[75] And yet she reacted against the notion of voluntary substitution which was approved in her convent and justified by a theory of merits. She preferred to lean on the theory of love. It was not a matter of putting oneself above others, but of drawing Christ to oneself in such a way as to draw him to all others.[76] A single hair of the beloved is enough to win the Bridegroom. There does not have to be any proportion between what one gives and what one receives from him. "So I ought to be satisfied to be your spouse," she said, "to be the mother of souls by my union with you."[77] And again:

> Jesus has made me understand this word of the Canticle: "Draw me: we will run after the odor of your perfumes. . . ." O Jesus, you did not have to say: "By drawing me, draw the souls that I love." The simple word "draw" is

---

72. These ideas have been developed, for example, by S. Moore, *God is a new language* (London, 1967).

73. Letter of July 16, 1962, on the occasion of the 4th centenary of the reform of Carmel, in *Documentation catholique* 59 (1962): 1162.

74. *Letter 114*, ed. *Lettres* (Paris, 1948), p. 205.

75. *Letter 74*, p. 135. The whole of this letter illustrates the reconciliation between the "desire" to "save souls" and the simple glance toward Jesus. "He desires only a look, a sigh, but a look and a sigh for him alone."

76. Witnessed for example—whatever the interpretations that accompany the quotations—by the texts collected by M. Moré, "La table des pécheurs" in *Dieu vivant* 24 (1953): 15-103.

77. *History of a Soul*, ch. 11.

enough, Lord, and I understand. When a soul has let itself be captivated by the inebriating odor of your per-
fumes, it cannot run alone. All the souls that it loves are
drawn after it. There is no constraint about this, no effort. It is the natural result of its attraction for you.[78]

Finally, Elizabeth of the Trinity. It has been said of her:

This love which is God and which God dispenses is, by
its simple presence, a purifying and redemptive power.
Anything that is not holy is sanctified by its presence
and contact. This is the strength, the radiance, the apostolate of divine love. By sharing in this power of love the
purified and sanctified soul is given the same power. Being
present to him who is present to her, she is touched by
a ray of divine light, and like it, she herself is communicated: "You are the light of the world." Elizabeth praises
with the same vigor as little Thérèse the apostolic character of love, and of life wholly offered and immolated
in God's service, and is clearly writing in the Carmelite
tradition. "I would want to be all silence, all worship so
as to enter even more into him and be so filled with him
that I can give him by prayer to those little souls who do
not know the gift of God!"

She writes to a priest:

"I want to be an apostle like you, from the heart of my
dear solitude in Carmel. I want to work for the glory of
God, and that means that I must be filled with him. Then
I will be all-powerful: one look, one wish becomes an ir-
resistible prayer that can obtain all, since it is, so to speak,
God who offers it to God." She wanted to be like a small
vessel at the source and fountain of life, to communicate
it to souls by letting its waves of infinite love overflow.[79]

This conception of the contemplative apostolate has prompted the following commentary:

Life is service, but so is theology service, and so is mysticism service. This fact was still clear at the end of the

---

78. *Autobiographical Manuscripts*, Ms C, Fol. 34.
79. H. U. von Balthazar, *Elizabeth de la Trinité et sa mission spirituelle* (Paris, 1959), p. 178.

patristic era, overflowing from the Gospel through a neo-platonic vision of the world, and now, after long centuries of egocentric asceticism and in the heart of this modern era of psychology, it must be rediscovered as the Catholic attitude deriving from revelation.

Elizabeth insists on the character of function and office. Office and charism are so similar in content that they overlap. Every charism in the Church is an office, and office in the pre-eminent order (like priesthood and hierarchy) are also a form of charismatic grace. In spite of all Elizabeth's respect for the priestly office, it is surprising to see how independent she is in her friendships with priests. She considers the office of the Carmelite as equivalent to that of the priest, each completing and complementing the other. She understood the Carmelite apostolate as the priestly apostolate. Both can radiate God, can give him to souls, by drawing from the divine source.[80]

CONCLUSION: PRESENCE AND AWARENESS

To live *for* the Church is first of all to live *with* her. Before one can share with others, one must receive a share oneself. One must become involved.

This reality becomes increasingly conscious, deliberate, intentional and explicit. Contemplatives are not always thinking of their neighbor. But when the chance comes along they must be ready to do so. Their continual state of communion has only to be actualized. The witness, the example, the contacts have not been sought, but neither have they been refused. By forgetting and emptying oneself, it becomes possible to draw and enlighten others in every way. One who prays habitually reveals God's presence. Action comes not from a pretense to influence nor by deliberate choice. It results from a profound inner conviction that the salvation of the universe does matter—and this conviction is only waiting for the chance to express and prove itself. Among contemplatives, there have always been some who have acted as spokesman for the common experience of all. They assure us that the only desire

80. *Ibid.,* pp. 184-185.

of contemplatives is for union with the Bridegroom. They read in his eyes his love for all men and feel called to herald this love, to proclaim and communicate it. Sometimes, as St Bernard admitted, they preferred to concentrate on him alone—but they heard the command to rise and share with others what they had received.[81] Their service of their neighbor overflowed from their enjoyment of God. They discover that the love hitherto confined in their own hearts is universal and needs to expand and to have scope for development. Active religious see their service of others as the way to union with God, but contemplatives have no intention beyond union with God, who has the right to send them to help their brothers for his sake.

There are very few who live exclusively for God in the world, but he himself has set aside some from whom he asks the extravagance of seeking himself alone. He can use them in the service of others, perhaps. But their communion with others depends first of all on their communion with him. By living in God's presence they make others present to God in themselves. A mere passing thought of their neighbor will be enough to prompt a prayer: *Memento Domine.* To pray is to consent to the design of salvation accomplished in Christ, to seek its greater fulfillment and contribute toward it. The more one prays the more is salvation furthered, both in oneself, and (still deeper at the heart of the mystery) in others.

This reality justifies today's "incarnational" vocabulary and its application to human relationships. It cannot be held, either for God in Christ or for the Christian in the world, that the incarnation is only or even primarily an insertion into the reality, that is entered and shared, for the purpose of acting upon it. Theological tradition speaks of *homo assumptus.* One does not equate oneself with what one assumes, but one raises it above itself, uniting it with oneself. In this sense, one raises a thing to the level of the world that is one's own by nature, while, however respecting the nature of the thing raised, for this nature is not destroyed but transformed. Hence,

81. *Sup. Cantica* 57:9-11; *S. Bernardi opera* 2:124-126; 18:3; *ibid.* 1:105; CF 4:135.

the Christian's duty—from which the contemplative is not
dispensed—is to understand the world, to embrace it and
then quite definitely to set out to raise the level of human
existence up to God in Christ and make it eschatological.
This "taking up" which makes the world present to God in
us is realised in many ways, amounting to so many forms of
the charity spread abroad in our hearts by the Spirit of the
risen Jesus: example, witness, teaching, service, intercession,
but primarily—and especially for those less given to activities
of immediate service—intense and deliberate responsibility and
solidarity with the depths of human misery by temptation
and suffering, with the hard social conditions of the poor,
with the aspirations of men for the God whom they so often
do not know but who seeks them and comes to meet them.
Christian contemplation, then, is purification as well as prayer.
It demands the sacrifice of all self-love. It opens the heart to
that form of presence to God which is responsibility-in-love.

CHAPTER VI

THE RELEVANCE OF THE CONTEMPLATIVE LIFE[1]

IN THE RESPONSES OF BOTH her leaders and members, the pilgrim Church, as we call her nowadays, sees the problem she has to face clarified. This is true in every domain, including religious life, and it is especially true in monastic and contemplative life. So, after having sought the "understanding of the Church" during the conciliar[2] and then during the post-conciliar period,[3] we perhaps need to ask ourselves today what it is after the first Synod of Bishops. One will see that some of the elements of solution came to light during the Synod itself and are showing up in many texts and documents.

CONTEMPLATION AND ATHEISM

On October 11, 1967, during the Synod's discussion on the problems concerning doctrine and faith, a group of contemplative monks addressed to the Synod "a message which is a testimony to the possibilities men have of entering into dialogue with the ineffable God who has revealed himself to his creatures."[4] The text was published on the following day.[5]

1. *Nouvelle revue théologique* 100 (1968), pp. 66-78.
2. Cf. "La vie contemplative et le monachisme d'après Vatican II" in *Aspects du monachisme,* pp. 11-37.
3. Cf. "Témoignages contemporains sur la théologie du monachisme," *ibid.,* pp. 99-133.
4. These were the formulas used in announcing the message in *L'Osservatore Romano* of Oct. 11, p. 2, and presenting it in that of Oct. 12, p. 2.
5. In *L'Osservatore Romano.* The text was read and published in French. It had already been printed by the Vatican Press, in a pamphlet of 12 pages, destined to

Its full meaning derived from its context, from the whole debate to which it was directed. It was a question of the dangers of atheism, which are the current preoccupation of the Church's pastors, and, in a more general way, the difficulties which some Christians are experiencing in their faith at a time of general doubt. Many of the bishops were of the opinion that it is not sufficient to denounce dangers and abuses, or to condemn errors where they appear. These held that one must bear positive witness to the faith. The authors of the Message had only this in mind: they said they wanted to make their "simple word" heard; they wanted to bear "witness," to show "the sympathy and understanding of the contemplative" for the sufferings of so many of his contemporaries. (The word *witness* was used three times, and the word *understanding* twice.)

The contemplatives were not concerning themselves with the doctrinal statements which pertain to the teaching authority of the bishops and the research of theologians, but with their "experience" (a word they use five times), and with "conscience." Their tone convinces the reader that such contemplative experience does exist and that these men have known it; and further, it shows that some of them in the name of all the rest have analysed the content of this problem and elaborated its phenomenology. Some of the wording is significantly reminiscent of the recent writings of Thomas Merton;[6] and elsewhere there are suggestions of an article by a Carthusian.[7] Here in the Message, as with both these modern

be distributed by the Holy Father himself, under the title *"Message of the Contemplative Monks to the Synod of Bishops on the Possibility of Man's Dialogue with the Ineffable God"* (September, 1967). This date seems to indicate that the text had been divulged and approved in advance. It was read to the Synod by Bishop Charrière of Lausanne, Geneva and Fribourg—in whose diocese the Chartreuse of Valsainte is to be found—and it was "welcomed with great applause," reports *L'Osservatore* of the 11th. The paper adds "A brief letter, addressed to the Holy Father and read by the Secretary General, explains the spirit in which the 'Message' was written and delivered. This letter bears, in the name of all contemplative orders, the signature of the Minister General of the Grande Chartreuse and the Abbot of the Cistercians. Since then a "Note" on the genesis of the text has appeared in *Collectanea Cisterciensia* 29 (1967): 205.

6. "Christian Solitude. Notes on an Experiment" in *The Current* (Feb. 1967), pp. 23-28.

7. "Un Chartreux, Solitude et sainteté" in *La vie spirituelle* 103 (1960): 139-152, the conclusion pp. 150-152: "La vérité inexorable."

writers, the problem is not just stated in some abstract and impersonal way but grasped at its very roots, in the heart of man, and set forth in biblical phrasing—with much of the vocabulary of the temptation. This approach makes it possible to show from a theological point of view what there is in common in the spiritual order of which they speak for the world, the Christian and the contemplative.

> The world is tempted to give way to atheism, denying the God whom it cannot understand on his own level, since he does not come within the range of its scientific instruments or calculations. Even Christians are moved by concern to share fully the plight of their brothers and yield to similar feelings by praising the need for a kind of incredulity as the basis for fully human sincerity. . . .
> In the trials and temptations that are assailing other Christians, the contemplative can recognise himself. He understands these trials and can discern their meaning. . . . He can more easily understand how the temptation to atheism can ultimately have a salutary effect on the faith of certain Christians and act in a similar way as the night of the mystic. . . .

Now this is what disturbs so many of our contemporaries and rouses the pastoral solicitude of the Pope and Bishops. It is not necessarily a question of temptations *against faith,* but of temptations *in the faith,* or in the search for faith. "We refer especially to those difficulties in the faith which some Christians are now experiencing . . . those who are struggling hard to keep or to find faith in Jesus Christ . . . the trials of the faith in our own times. . . ." Now this notion of temptation and trial, and its whole reality, is part of the patrimony of earliest monastic tradition.[8] More recent mystical writers speak in terms of the "night" and our document echoes this: the contemplative "knows all the bitterness of the dark night." It is not so long ago since Thérèse of Lisieux lived through suffering like this.[9]

8. Texts dealing with ancient monachism are quoted for example in H. Dorries "Die Beichte im Alten Mönchtum" in *Studia Patristica* 3 (Berlin, 1962): 284-311, and in *Wort und Stunde* (Göttingen, 1966), pp. 225-250.

9. Proof of this is to be found for example in the pages where she describes the "mists," the "darkness," the "night," the "suffering," the "trial" that faith means for her. "It is no longer a veil for me, but a wall reaching to heaven." *Autobiographical manuscripts* (Lisieux, 1957), pp. 251-254.

Where are we to find the answer to this difficulty which is experienced in all its reality by Christians both in the world and in the cloister? We will get it from him who experienced and overcame the temptation before us and for us: "The Lord Jesus, after conquering the devil, showed the full extent of his power as the prelude to his paschal victory. . . ." The contemplative "knows also, through the life of Christ, that God is the vanquisher of death. The Lord was tempted in the desert but he overcame the tempter. Christ dies for our sins and rose again for our justification. . . ." Recent studies insist more and more on the importance of the temptation of Christ in early catechesis and theology.[10] Monks have always regarded the retreat of the Lord to the Mount of the Temptation as a kind of anticipated symbol of their own vocation; in this sense, one could quote many witnesses from early times,[11] as well as the medieval[12] and the modern periods. One of our contemporary Eastern monks has adopted a very provocative parallel between the temptations of Christ and those of the monk.[13] The monk is essentially a man under temptation.[14] This particular form of spiritual trial was considered as his speciality in earlier times: people would refer to the

10. A bibliography has been given by L. de Lorenzi, *La preghiera nella Bibbia e nella tradizione* (Rome, 1964), pp. 132-133. Since then there has appeared among others, J. Dupont, "L'origine du récit des tentations de Jésus au désert" in *Revue biblique* 73 (1966): 20-76.

11. In *Chances de la spiritualité occidentale* (Paris, 1966), pp. 251-252, I have quoted some texts. The parallel between the solitude of Christ in the desert and that of those who forsake the world has been often developed, sometimes at great length, by Philoxene de Marbourg, *Homilies* ed. E. Lemoine, *Sources chrétiennes* 44 (Paris, 1956), pp. 245-246, 253-258, 263-269, 271-288, 304. Cf. also, J. C. Guy "Le combat contre le démon dans le monachisme ancien" in *Assemblies du Seigneur* 30 (Bruges, 1964): p. 62.

12. For example, Hugues de Balma (Carthusian of the 13th century), *De mystica theologia,* ed. Peltier, *S. Bonaventurae opera* (Paris, Vives, 1966) 8:1-41. Other references in *Chances de la spiritualité,* pp. 271-272. R. E. M. Nally, "The Pseudo-Isidorian de vetere et Novo Testamento quaestiones" in *Traditio* 19 (1963): 49, no. 50.

13. P. Evdokimov, *Les âges de la vie spirituelle* (Paris, 1964), pp. 127-133: "Les trois tentations, les trois réponses, et les trois voeux monastiques."

14. The expression figured in the title of an article by J. Guitton, "Il monaco uomo tentato?" in *L'Osservatore Romano* of Jan. 28, 1967. But there it was question of the temptations the monk might experience against his vocation, in particular that of doing something other than leading the monastic life.

"temptations of monks"[15] in the context of the various types of authentic human suffering which Christians had to undergo, and which varied with the state of life. The authors of the Message of the Contemplatives to the Synod of Bishops echo this constant tradition: by vocation and by experience they know how insupportable suffering can be.

So they do have something to say about it. They have withdrawn from the world not to keep themselves aloof from it but to be one with it. What is true of other periods remains true of our own. In relation to the expansion of monasticism in Africa, someone has recently written: "A monk is a man of the desert, but he is also the brother of all those who still live in the world. The monk withdraws to the desert in order to encounter God—in the same way as Jesus himself withdrew to the desert and the entire people of God wandered for forty years in the desert. But for all that, the monk does not forget his brothers; he loves them, prays for them and knows how to serve them. In the heart of the Sahara Charles de Foucauld earned the title 'brother of the whole world.' It was this conviction[17] that persuaded the authors of the message to intervene: "As a group of contemplative monks we feel that we are one with our bishops in their pastoral preoccupations. . . . We do not want to deprive ourselves in the name of silence and solitude of what could be a chance to serve our brothers. . . . Our message could be useful to God's people and to the world of today. . . . For we are united with the whole Church and associated in the world's suffering. . . ."

If the contemplative withdraws from the world, he does not desert it, or desert his brothers either. He remains ever rooted in the world where he was born, for he has in-

15. "There come to mind the wretched condition of the poor, the tears of orphans, the desolation of widows . . . the temptations of monks, the sollicitude of prelates, . . ." Aelred of Rievaulx, *Rule of Life for a Recluse,* ch. 28; ed. C. Dumont, *Sources chrétiennes* 76 (Paris, 1961), p. 112; CF 2:77-78.

16. F. Louvel "En 20 ans 32 monastères" in *La vie spirituelle* 110 (1964): 465. Cf. "L'avenir des moines" in *Aspects du Monachisme,* pp. 181-187: "Solitude monastique et solidarité d'Église."

17. E.g., "The wise man can never be alone: he has with him all those who are and those who have been good . . ."—St Jerome, *Adv. Jovinianum* 1:47; PL 23:273, quoting Theophrastes.

herited its riches and has made a genuine attempt to take up its preoccupations and aspirations. The on-going drive of the world has a divine source and the contemplative tries to recollect himself more deeply at this source and in its light to understand the deep design of man. In fact, it is in the desert that the loftiest inspirations sometimes come to the soul. It was in the desert that God fashioned his people, and after their fall it was to the desert that he led them "to win them back to himself and speak to their heart." (Hos 11:16) . . . The rebirth and renewal of God's people in each generation is an experience analogous to this.

The contemplative becomes involved through this under-standing of communion, through his need for solidarity—in a word, through charity. This feature is constant throughout tradition. It is found in early times as well as medieval[18] and modern.[19] And the authors of the Message add a motive which clearly indicates their grounds for speaking today:

> The contemplative life in monasteries is nothing other than the simple Christian life, lead in conditions that foster the "experience" of God. One could even speak of specialization in the relationship with God, which places us in a position to give a witness in regard to this.

We can recognize here the notion of specialization on which Paul VI recently insisted.[20] Because the contemplative is in

18. See, for example, the texts quoted by C. Hallet, "La Communion des personnes d'après un oeuvre de Baudouin de Ford" in *Revue d'ascétique et de mystique* 42 (1966): 405-432. "Contemplative life is therefore to possess whole-heartedly the love of God and neighbor." John de Kastl, ed. J. Sudbrack *Die geistliche Theologie des Johannes von Kastl* (Munich, 1967) 2:135, no. 152.

19. "Solitude is not merely a negative relationship. It is not merely the absence of people. True solitude is a participation in the solitariness of God—Who is in all things. His solitude is not a local absence but a metaphysical transcendence. His solitude is his Being. For us, solitude is not a matter of being something more than other men, except by accident; for those who cannot be alone find their true being and they are always something less than themselves. For us solitude means a withdrawal from an artificial and fictional level of being which men, divided by original sin, have fabricated in order to keep pace with concupiscence and death. But by that very fact the solitary finds himself on the level of a more spiritual society—the city of those who have become real enough to confess and glorify God (that is: life), in the teeth of death. Solitude and society are formed and perfected in the Sacrifice of the Mass."—Th. Merton, *The Sign of Jonas* (New York: Harcourt, Brace, 1963), p. 269.

20. Cf. "Témoignages contemporains," *loc. cit.*, pp. 112-113.

a way a professional in the darksome search for God,[21] he shares intensely in the joy and pain that go to make up faith. His experience does not seem esoteric but typical of all Christian experience. It is really beyond description, but Paul, John and the other apostles showed that it is the basic experience of every Christian. . . . Here again we have the echo of a spiritual tradition in which the monks of all times have felt themselves at home. It is common knowledge that modern theology gives renewed importance to the analysis of religious experience as we have it in God's witnesses in the Old and New Testament, and right through the history of the Church.[22] Someone has written: "Contemplation begins the moment when God's presence and action in us, and our life in Christ, have fully rectified and scattered all that opposes or hinders it. What we hitherto searched for in a dark and obscure way now becomes the object of our experience. This experience is very mysterious no doubt and yet very real; more real, in fact, than our sensory experience or ordinary intellectual activity."[23] With a man like St Bernard, you find that this experience is the foundation of all his teaching.[24] And there are countless examples that we could bring forth from monastic history.[25]

But let there be no misunderstanding; spiritual experience is not only experience of God, it is also and primarily experience of man with all the poverty that belongs to his condition. It is man's knowledge of himself in the presence of God, man's awareness of needing God, which he himself puts in our hearts; it is man's incapacity to satisfy this need without God, and man's difficulty in satisfying this need even with God's help. It is purifying experience. [The Holy Father writes:]

21. Cf. "L'Avenir des moines," *loc. cit.,* pp. 172-173.

22. In proof of this see the great work of H. Urs von Balthasar, *La gloire et la croix. Les aspects esthétiques de la Révélation. I: Apparition* (Paris, 1965) ch. 2: *L'expérience de foi,* pp. 185-360.

23. L. Bouyer, *Introduction à la vie spirituelle* (Paris: Desclée et Cie, 1960), p. 82.

24. Under the title "S. Bernard et l'expérience chrétienne" in *Aspects du Monachisme,* I have assembled the texts.

25. See for example, A. Hallier "L'expérience spirituelle selon Aelred de Rievaulx" in *Collectanea Ord. Cist. Ref.* 20 (1958), 97-113 and the articles of D. P. Miguel appearing there in 1965 and 1967, in *Irenikon* of 1964 to 1967, and "Spécificité et caractères de l'expérience spirituelle chez Aelred de Rievaulx" in *Collectanea Cisterciensia* 29 (1967): 3-11.

The desert lays our heart open; it uncovers our pretexts, our alibis, our imperfect images of God. It reduces us to the essential, corners us in our own truth and leaves no loophole for flight. This may be beneficial even for our faith; it is, then, in the depth of our poverty that the marvels of God's mercy are manifest and in the depth of our sluggishness that we find grace, the extraordinary strength of God, "which is perfected only in weakness" (2 Cor 12:9) . . . Our faith is always in need of being cleansed and detached from all the false images that we set up in its stead—but the night of the faith opens into the unshakable certainty placed in our hearts by the very God who chose to try us.

There is a very positive value in all this and out witness may:

. . . become a word of comfort and hope. If it passes along desert ways, very similar to the temptations of atheism, the experience of the contemplative is not negative: the absence of the transcendent God is also, by paradox, his imminent presence. Perhaps recollection, silence, withdrawal from some of the disturbances of life are necessary if we are to perceive him; in this sense, we are the privileged ones. But every Christian is called to taste God. This is a fact that we want to proclaim, for it warns man against any kind of lassitude or pessimism that would engender a less happy outlook in this regard, than we enjoy.

We see that if the contemplative is in one way a specialist in the trial of faith, he is a specialist also in the joy that gives rise to hope, to eschatological longing and to the "encounter with personal love." So he can speak of "joy", "thanksgiving" and "wonder."

Our message can conclude only on a note of gratitude. This is the sentiment that is always uppermost on one who has experienced the infinite generosity of God. The Christian is a sinner who has been pardoned, he is the object of God's mercy in a completely unexpected way, "sharing the lot of the saints in light" (Col 1:12) and can remain in God's presence only if he echoes continually the song of thanksgiving: "For he is good, and his love without end." (Ps 136)

The final sentence introduces a new note: the authors of the Message invite all their brethren to share with them and cultivate the seeds of heavenly contemplation sown in their heart. We have had other references to the contemplative, but the term contemplation is today being contested and is here avoided deliberately. After all that has been said of the knowledge and love of God in biblical language, in the light of quotations from Scripture which have not all been cited in the extracts given here, it is clear that the contemplation which, in the obscurity of faith makes us sharers in the dialogue between Father and Son in the Holy Spirit, and which will be achieved in the glory of the risen life, is a Christian reality; there is nothing neo-platonic about it. Finally, let us note that, except in the first sentence, where contemplative monks are mentioned, there is no monastic reference. We find "contemplative life in cloisters," "cloistered life" and "desert"— in the sense in which this word is used in tradition. But since the word *monk* is now applied to others besides contemplatives, it seems best to be discreet in its use.[26]

STUDIES AND PRIESTHOOD

A few days after the reading of the Message of the Contemplatives, the Synod of Bishops heard a new presentation concerning them in the course of a discussion on seminaries. Here is a summary of it published in the press:

> Theology assumes a special aspect when it is joined to contemplation. Some monks quite legitimately devote themselves to apostolic activities and on that account could be formed somewhat along the same lines as the secular clergy. But the monk who is entirely devoted to contemplation needs an absolutely special theological formation. Let the competent authorities take account of the variety of charisms lest they deprive monks of this special formation which is essential to the full development of their vocation.[27]

26. This was also the course adopted in the article which has become the preceding chapter of this volume.
27. Italian text in *L'Osservatore Romano*, October 16-17, 1967, p. 5.

Almost at the same time an article appeared by Father Jean Beyer SJ treating of the same problem. The Dean of the Faculty of Canon Law at the Gregorian University gave proof of deep understanding of the monastic vocation and of its needs in the field of institutions. He demanded that a special plan of studies be established in our days by the monks themselves, and this was his reason.

> Studies are absolutely necessary if monks are to take their contemplative life seriously. . . . Now it is not only a matter of studies preparatory to the priesthood. This problem touches the very nature and quality of the monastic vocation. . . . If this vocation is correctly understood theologically it is entirely consecrated to the contemplation of divine mysteries . . . it may be followed either eremitically or cenobitically. Such a goal cannot be reached without the study of Holy Scripture, of revealed truth, the dogmas of the Catholic faith, without understanding of the divine praise and preparing for the monastic office. This general formation, acquired in the monastery is carried on at all times, and must be common for all the monks. . . . It makes one pass from spiritual reading to theological study which, although speculative, must always remain different from what is taught in seminaries and faculties of theology; it must truly foster the unity of the monastic life and never lose sight of the goal of this life, which is the search for God. . . . It must, then, have the great dogmas of the faith as its object, for these are the foundations of prayer and contemplation, true aids to a monastic life lived in its fullness. And the manner of studying must, so to speak, fill the mind and heart of the monk with divine light thanks to which he will devote himself to prayer more easily, more deeply and more fruitfully. Thus we see clearly why monastic studies do not consist primarily in research of a critical nature, but in "sapiential" and abiding understanding, an assiduous penetration into the mystery of God, which, in order to carry through with greater fidelity and reverence, will use for its own ends and with discretion, the scientific means prepared by others. . . . If these studies are to foster peace of soul, they need to be spread out over each man's whole lifetime. . . .

Besides the principal questions, several other things will also be taught, especially to those who are being prepared with a view to the priesthood, not as a preparation for pastoral functions but as a means of formation for their own kind of life. . . . Many advantages will result for the whole Church from the renewal of monastic studies: a greater sense of the divine presence, a deeper knowledge of the mysteries of God, better conditions for monastic prayer and the peacefulness of the whole cenobitic life.[28]

Father Beyer goes into details which this short analysis does not give. And he concludes with a vigorous resumé of the concept of monasticism underlying his whole argument:

If knowledge of the world does not rest on contemplation of God it can turn monasteries away from their religious meaning: they become houses of apostolic institutes, or simply places of cohabitation for religious who, at fixed hours, once they have carried out some form of liturgical celebration, devote themselves to human and profane works which may have a scientific, technical or artistic character, or satisfy the daily necessities, but not religious who preserve a monastic life that is integrally oriented to the search for God.[29]

The Message of the Contemplatives included no reference to the priesthood. This might have limited it to monks only, and to a single category of them, excluding nuns altogether. Father Beyer has shown that the problem of studies is primarily the same for all men and women living the contemplative life. As for the priesthood of monks, it is a question that is still being studied, either in the name of "a theology which makes a broad appeal to reasons of appropriateness,"[30] or in the light of history.[31] The most recent opinion expressed on this subject

28. J. Beyer, "Decretum *Perfectae Caritatis* Concilii Vaticani II (Commentarium, pars V)" in *Periodica de re morali, canonica, liturgica* 56 (1967): 532-534.

29. *Ibid.*, p. 535.

30. The expression is found in *Collectanea Cisterciensia* 29 (1967): 28, in a series of reports of publications on the priesthood of monks. Since then has appeared the animated note of D. G. Frenand "Vie monastique et sacerdoce" in *Gregorianum* 48 (1967): 588-595.

31. A very just focusing on this is given by Fr Martin de Elizade, "El sacerdocio de los Monjes" in *Cuadernos monasticos* 3 (1967): 93-125.

sums up many others: "One can say with assurance nothing
has changed the character of the monastic life as much as the
broad increase of the ministerial priesthood, which is not
even necessary for the duties of teaching."[32]

CHARISM AND INSTITUTION

Father Beyer asked that monks should be able to determine
their own program of studies, and thus resolve for themselves
the problem of their formation and at the Synod it had been
suggested that the variety of charisms in this field be respected.
The same principle should be applied to all points which concern the different forms of the contemplative life. In his address to the World Congress on the Apostolate of the Laity,
October 15, 1967, Paul VI said of St Teresa of Avila: "We
are thinking of giving her, and St Catherine of Siena, the title
of Doctor of the Church one day."[33] Now St Teresa taught
nothing except mystical theology; though she excelled equally
in constitutional law. She concretized her spiritual doctrine
in a collection of observances which she gathered into Constitutions and which she considered to be the necessary conditions for the contemplative life which she had the charism to
introduce—or restore—in the Church. The history of the vicissitudes of this legislative work shows that it was not, during
the Saint's life and after, always understood by the religious
who were not living the life that she wished for herself and
her daughters. We have an important lesson here: can one
legislate for a kind of life if one has not lived it?

Once again, history comes to the help of theology here,
by showing how, in practice, institutions are born and grow
in the Church. Fr Ghislain Lafont has devoted to this problem
a study that is well developed, deep, precise and penetrating.
Two extracts will suffice.

> On its own, spiritual doctrine cannot regulate, even briefly,
> a form of common life nor can a juridical constitution

32. B. Webb, Review of C. Cary-Elwes, *Monastic Renewal* in *The Downside
Review* 85 (1967): 432.
33. Text in *L'Osservatore Romano* of Oct. 16-17, 1967, p. 2.

deprived of doctrinal support and an evangelical basis give spiritual dignity to this form of life. Both are necessary. Ancient monastic rules are a good example of this point: without break in continuity they develop an ascetic doctrine that is whole and entire, directly and expressly drawn from Scripture, a system of government and forms of common life that are oriented toward the development, and success, of the proposed ascesis. In the Rule of St Benedict we can no more do without Chapter 7 on humility than we can do without Chapter 2 and 64 on the abbot, or the chapters on food, drink or work. It is the whole Rule that holds and defines spiritually and concretely the monastic charism, preserved by the Holy Spirit in the Church to serve as the spirituality for the desert and the time of waiting. . . .

It is clear, then, that in this context "charismatic" and "juridical" are not opposite designations. On the contrary, the charism of institution relates to the organic community and to the expression of its basic laws: a particular law results which is only the universal and written code for the institution that is willed and preserved by the Holy Spirit. A juridical element forms part of the inner essence of a religious family willed by God; it is united to the doctrinal elements from which it flows and allows this family to be collectively faithful to its own characteristic Gospel inspiration and thus to contribute to the evangelical life of the whole Church.[34]

EXIGENCIES AND SIGNS OF RENEWAL

Catholic monasticism is not alone in facing these problems or in trying to solve them. But it is a groping process and holds out no promise of quick, easy solution. The questions relating to forms of contemplative life were dealt with lucidly and humbly by the representatives of other Christian churches and communities at the Ecumenical Congress on Renewal in the Religious Life held at Ramegnies-Chin, in the diocese of Tournai, in April, 1967, and also at the Conference of Angli-

---

34. "L'Esprit Saint et le droit dans l'institution religieuse" in *La vie spirituelle: Supplément,* 82 (September, 1967), 488 and 490.

can Religious which took place at Oxford in the following July. It is clear that there are two facts calling for attention from all sides.

First of all, conditions in today's world and Church bring contemplatives face to face with new exigencies which they will be able to meet only by fidelity to their respective traditions and by the spirit of inventiveness: the first will ensure that this tradition will be a true transmission to the present and the future of the heritage received from the great charismatics of the past. But fidelity is not all. There is clearly a perceptible renewal of the contemplative ideal and here we have an unquestionable sign of the vitality of Christianity today, and reason for hope in the future.

At the World Council for the Apostolate of the Laity, a Catholic woman "asked to speak about 'contemplation' as an experience contributing here and now to the salvation of the world. In very telling words she observed that the life of prayer—which takes for granted silence, interior life and peace— is not incompatible with temporal and social involvement." Her "witness" was greatly applauded.[35] Members of cloistered contemplative institutes must rejoice in these calls to the contemplative life in the world: for they show that there are two different realizations of the same aspiration which the Holy Spirit preserves and revives in the Church, and these go hand in hand, each complementing the other. On behalf of the Church of England, Doctor Ramsay had already emphasized this. In words that are worthy to be quoted by way of conclusion, the Archbishop of Canterbury stated: "I wish to point out again a fact which is a tremendous encouragement for us, and a source of hope. . . . A great movement is afoot—the renewal of the contemplative life. We see it in the appearance of specifically contemplative orders for both men and women; but we see it also in a broader dimension: in the renewed feeling of the Christian people that contemplation is not something strange or exaggerated, but a normal and sane reality, a prerogative belonging to every man in that he is a child of God. . . . I think that contemplative prayer consists

35. From *L'Osservatore Romano* of Oct. 13, 1967, p. 3.

only in having a tremendous desire for God. . . . Let us thank him for this renewal of the contemplative spirit."[36]

Finally, here are some thoughts which a Christian woman engaged in the study of "the consequences of the great new technology," has presented as "the reflection of a layman." In a chapter on the role and the tasks which men of God are called to assume today, she thus described the role of monasticism:

> For utility, it substitutes gratuity. For strength and power, the apparent weakness of prayer and sacrifice. For confidence in self, in reason and in human means, it substitutes trust in God and in his love. For increasing needs, as well as for the upheavals which they cause and the practical conditions which they effect, it substitutes poverty. But also the freedom of "full being." To the rumpus and tooting of the world, to restlessness and distraction, its reply is silence. And to human construction, it replies with the mystery of life in God.
> This kind of balance seems to be all the more necessary because of the gradual invasion of the world by the growing materialism of technology and finance. Men live in a whirlwind of false needs. Our era is losing a sense of values and an appreciation of authentic criteria, so that humanity is heading for self destruction instead of self fulfillment.
> Like an oasis round a spring in the heart of a desert, a monastery preserves a bond with the essential and a life deriving from it. It stands for a priority of values. Need is not avoided but faced. Wisdom expands to its fullest in sanctity. . . .[37]
> Good vocations persist among our young people, and visits to monasteries multiply. This would seem to justify monastic life more than ever. Monasteries belong to the full life of the Church since they are oases of prayer and contemplation. Priests and members of the hierarchy are attracted to this type of life, and even laymen who have had the chance of genuine contact with an abbey. All rediscover there the right priority of problems and situations.

36. Text in the *Cowley Evangelist* (July, 1966), pp. 102-103.

Monasteries continue, and will continue to play an important role. Perhaps it could be amplified in the present phase of history, for humanity needs to face up again to the essentials if it does not wish to die spiritually. . . .[38]

Any perception or understanding of situations, problems and needs, both in the West and beyond it, shows how necessary it is for monks and monasteries to play a more important role in the years to come. They need to find new ways and means of expressing God. They need to recall to the world, more insistently than ever, the values which it is forgetting and neglecting.

Above all, monasteries must beware of losing touch. If the world should become just one immense auto-regulated and calculated mechanism, if man becomes conditioned and the person robotized, monks will have lost their chance to get across. It will be too late . . .

The sciences and advanced techniques are leaving their marks on the world, and could very easily deform it. It is all the more urgent, then, for some to bear witness. It is an act of love to prepare for this witness—and more, it is the only way in which we can speak of God today and sing his praise, with any chance of being heard, listened to and followed. . . .[39]

37. Michele Aumont, *L'Église écoute. Réflexion de laïc* (Paris, 1967), p. 169. The authoress, who has written several works particularly concerning the condition of women in industrial society, is a counsellor for *CTN* (study center of the general consequences of the new techniques).

38. *Ibid.,* p. 173.

39. *Ibid.,* p. 180.

CHAPTER VII

CONFESSION AND THE PRAISE OF GOD

CONTEMPLATIVE LIFE, RELIGIOUS LIFE—indeed Christian life itself, all have a penitential character. Essentially this penance is the same for all members of the Church. We recognize and acknowledge ourselves as sinners, and strive to weaken our tendency to sin by mortification and self-denial. The aim in all this is to make one's search for God more intense, more exclusive and more efficacious. Penance assumes a particular character in contemplative life because this life is characterized by the continuity of its search for God.

The Message of the Contemplatives to the Synod of Bishops[1] made this point clear. Penitence, however, is not morbid pleasure in some sort of guilt complex. Rather, it is grounded on faith in the mystery of sin and forgiveness, on the hope of salvation which God gives us in Christ and on the love which the Spirit pours into our hearts. It is expressed in prayer. It wells up into praise and thanksgiving. In fact, our spirit of prayer can be gauged by our spirit of penance. A good measure of prayer shows a good measure of penance. This penance itself is characterized by gratitude and joy as well as by humble confession and asceticism. The Council combines both aspects in its reference to "ready penance" carried out in a spirit of joyous enthusiasm.

We are not concerned here with the whole mystery of penance but with one of its expressions incumbent on all Chris-

1. See above, pp. 96ff.

108

tians: humble confession especially in the relationship to the praise of God.[2] We shall touch on the confession of faults in monasteries and convents, as a spiritual problem of the practical order.

* * * * * *

Many Christians participate with fervor in penitential celebrations—a fact which gives the lie to any talk about a contemporary "crisis of penance." Within the Church, the Holy Spirit is keeping souls alert to the inner meaning of this reality of penance.

On the other hand there is no doubt about the "crisis of confession." We need to understand it though, before we begin our lament. Possibly it originates in the over-restricted notion sometimes given to confession as a specific act of penance: the limitation of the whole to one of its aspects brings the accompanying risk of over-emphasis. The solution may lie in the full biblical and traditional dimension of confession, with stress on its theological importance. Such a change would show that penance is an act of worship; whatever its form, it belongs as a part of the liturgy. To separate the negative element, as one speaks of it today, is to diminish both. This negative element consists in the acknowledgement of sin, accompanied by sorrow. The positive element in praise of God in the joy of the Holy Spirit. The history of the word "confession" throws light on this. We give it briefly.[3]

THE OLD TESTAMENT

The classical Latin for the words confess (*confiteri*) and confession (*confessio*)[4] have the same double application: the proclamation or declaration of truth and the acknowledgement or admission of faults or guilt. Christians adopted both

2. This Chapter appeared in *La vie spirituelle* 118 (1968): 263-265.
3. The most recent study with reference to former publications, is that of G. Q. A. Meershoek, *Le Latin biblique d'après saint Jérôme* (Nijmegen, 1966), pp. 67-85.
4. Cf. *Thesaurus Linguae latinae*, (Leipzig, 1904-1909) 4:188-191 (*confessio*) and 226-233 (*confiteor*).

meanings. Confessing God, or his name, and confessing the faith indicates the public manifestation of fidelity to them, even at the cost of life. So the death of a martyr signifies confession in a special way. His burial place was called simply his "confession."[5] When confession of sins is meant, this was usually made explicit: "to confess one's sins" or "one's sinfulness."

However, the Bible introduced a third meaning for these same terms—one that was quite new and that was to occupy a large place in the vocabulary of prayer, as it did in the vocabulary of Old Testament worship.[6] *Confiteri*, meaning praise and thanksgiving, translates the Hebrew word *hôdeho* a word used in biblical poetry and especially in the Psalm to mean a sacrifice of thanksgiving. The chants accompanying this sacrifice expressed gratitude to God and described the trial one had endured. If the plight from which God had freed one or all of his people was caused by sin, this fact was also mentioned. Perhaps sacrifice had been promised under the duress of sin, sickness, imminent death, war or defeat. Then it would be confession twice over, for it recognized the greatness of the Lord as Savior and the misery of man in need of help. It is sometimes said that the praise needs to be expressed by a new canticle, hitherto unsung and inspired now directly by God. And it needs the accompaniment of music. So in Psalm 32:2-3, we have:

> "Give thanks to Yahweh on the harp:
> Rejoice unto him with a ten-stringed lyre.
> Sing him a new song!"

and in Psalm 38:4:

> "He has put into my mouth a new song, praise to our God!"

This is the meaning we give to the "Confessions of Jeremiah," signifying supplication and praise rather than admission of guilt.[7] Moreover, among the penitential psalms there are

---

5. Cf. C. Mohrmann, *Études sur le latin des chrétiens* (Rome, 1958) 1:31.

6. Cf. Michel in Kittel, *Theologisches Wörterbuch zum Neuen Testament* (Stuttgart, 1954) 5:202-205.

7. G. M. Behler, *Les confessions de Jérémie* (Casterman, 1959).

psalms expressing thanksgiving, prayer for divine mercy or gratitude.[8] From this point of view, the *Miserere* is more a Psalm of joy than of sorrow.[9] Self-accusation has its place but is swallowed up in praise of him in whose sight one has sinned:

> You are just when you accuse: without reproach when you judge.
> You love truth in the heart.
> Give me joy and thanksgiving.
> Give me the joy of your salvation.
> Lord, open my lips and my mouth will declare your praise. . . .
> (Psalm 50:6, 8, 10, 14, 17)

The Hebrew word meaning song of thanksgiving was translated in the Greek of the Septuagint by *exomologesthai*, and in the Latin by *confiteri, confessio.*

CHRISTIAN ANTIQUITY

The New Testament preserves the two meanings of *confiteri-confessio* from classical Latin, together with the third meaning found in biblical poetry. These words are now applied to man's relations with God in Christ Jesus. It is Christ who is praised and Christ to whom witness is given. Sins committed are confessed to be forgiven by his grace.[10] These two meanings converge in the connotation specific to the third: profession of faith and admission of sin are made in thanksgiving to the Father. Through the incarnate Son and the Spirit whom he sends, the Father saves man by forgiveness. This full meaning of the word *confessio* was maintained and developed right through patristic tradition, from Antiquity to the early Middle Ages.

Origen's Greek equivalents for *confiteri* express praise, worship, gratitude and also acknowledgement and admission of

8. G. Bernini, *Le preghiere penitenziali del Salterio* (Rome: Pont. Univ. Gregoriana, 1953).

9. Cf. C. Augrain, *Témoins de l'Esprit* (Paris: Cerf, 1966), p. 59.

10. Cf. "Confession" in X. Leon-Défour, *Vocabulaire de théologie biblique* (Paris: Cerf, 1962), pp. 150-152.

sin. Moreover, the Greek Fathers of the fourth and fifth centuries—Athanasius, Basil, Chrysostom, Cyril of Alexandria and
others—also preserve these two aspects of the Christian approach. By confessing our sins to God we glorify him. Monasticism has helped to preserve and spread this full meaning of
confession. It fostered the element of self-accusation, giving
expression to a practice common among Christians.[11]

Bishops and preachers also used the same idea and the same
terms of reference in their pastoral teaching on sin and forgiveness. They use derivatives of confession to show the double
exigency of praise of God and admission of guilt both belonging to Christian life. They were ever exhorting the faithful to
reflect on the truths inherent in confession as an act of faith,
prayer and humility.[12]

In the Latin tradition, the Psalms provided ample opportunity for enlarging on the twofold duty of thanksgiving and
confession. The word *confiteri* is in constant use. In a commentary on Psalm 135:1 *"Confitemini Domino quoniam
bonus . . .,"* St Jerome exclaims: "Here, confession is used
in the sense of praise." He then quotes a verse from the New
Testament which he and others compare with Old Testament
references using the same term: "I give thanks to you, Lord,
Father of heaven and earth . . . (Mt 11:25). Now, Christ could
not confess sins. He could not confess except in praise.[13] In
the same way, among Christian titles to the Psalms we find
"The voice of Christ confessing God's almighty power."[14] And
further on, "In this psalm the people are called to confession,
that they may remember the Lord and his marvels."[15]

St Augustine expressed the same approach to the Psalms
with characteristic intensity:

> You praise God when you accuse yourself. In fact, his
> mercy is the forgiveness of your sins. Acknowledgement
> of sins contributes to your praise of God. It is the very

11. Cf. G. Couilleau, "Accusation de soi dans le monachisme antique" in *La
vie spiritualle* 117 (1967): 309-314.

12. Cf. G. Q. A. Meershoek, *op. cit.*, p. 77.

13. *Commentarium in Ps.* 1; CC 72:241, quoted by Meershoek, p. 69.

14. Ed. P. Salmon, *Les "tituli Psalmorum" des manuscrits latins* (Rome, 1959),
pp. 92-138.

15. *Ibid.,* pp. 91, 135.

apex of praise. The deeper our despair in illness, the greater our praise of the one who cures it.[16]
A little thought suffices to show that self-reproach is actually praise of God. Confession of sin constitutes praise of God, because from death you have come to life again. And if you are raised to life by confession of sin, who has raised you? Confession does indeed comprise accusation of self and praise of God.... Whether we accuse ourselves or praise God, we still praise him doubly. By sincerity in self-accusation we praise him. By the fact of being our own accusers we praise him through whom we are restores to life....[17]
Always be your own accuser, then you will have no dearth of subject-matter. No conversion is ever so complete that there is no further cause for self-reproach. Accuse yourself; otherwise your judge will accuse you. When you come to the Lord's temple remember your own guilt. When can we have done with confession of sins? Only in the repose we are to share with the angels. But notice that I said "confession" for there will always be the confession of praise. You will be confessing for all eternity that God is God and you are his creature, that he is your protector and you, the one protected.[18]

St Augustine provides a fine example of both types of confession in the work called by that very name, *Confessions*. It begins with the words: "You are great, O Lord, and greatly to be praised.... Man wants to praise you ... you prompt him to seek his happiness in praising you...."[19] Later in his life he refers to this work in his *Revisions*: "The thirteen books of my Confessions praise you, God, because I have done both good and evil...."[20] The praise prompted by evil is an avowal. That prompted by good is gratitude. Recent research has shown that the notion contained in the word and

16. *In Ps.* 94:4; CC 39:1333.
17. *Sermo LXVII* 2-4; PL 38:433-444.
18. *In Ps. IC* 16; CC 39:1403-1410. Other texts on *Confiteri* in St Augustine are quoted by C. Vagaggini, "La teologia della lode secondo S. Agostino", in C. Vagaggini and C. Penco, *La preghiera nella Biblia e nella teologia* (Rome, 1964), pp. 435-439.
19. *Conf.* I, 1, 1; CSEL 33:1.
20. *Retract.* II, 6, 1; CSEL 36:137.

idea of confession, in this book of St Augustine, is that of sacrifice, and more precisely "sacrifice of praise."[21] The context
nearly always has a liturgical tone. He speaks of "offering" a
"sacrifice of praise," of "giving thanks"—the confession itself
is a "thank-offering." All this involves St Augustine's conception of sacrifice as the pre-eminent means of union with God.[22]
Since man is a sinner, this union is realized only by reconciliation with God, through conversion and return to him. The
only sacrifice that could unite mankind to God was that of
Jesus Christ: the efficacy of all other sacrifices derive from
this.

To confess God is to come back to his light from the "region
of unlikeness" where sin had kept us at a distance from him.
"Even sins (*etiam peccata*) are the occasion and condition of
praise."[23] Avowal and thanksgiving are intrinsic to the very
idea of confession as an act of worship. This word with its
rich significance of two complementary and inseparable realities was to pass into liturgical use. In the *Te Deum* we sing:
"We praise you, O God, we confess you to be Lord," and in
the ancient Terce hymn: "May our mouths, our tongues, our
spirits, our senses, our energy be made to confess. . . ."[24] The
missal provides other examples of this use of the word,[25] and
in the old Lenten hymn for Matins, the "renewal" effected by
forgiveness is linked up with the "new song."[26]

THE MIDDLE AGES

The first monastic rules of the West in the sixth and seventh
centuries preserve the two meanings of confession. Sometimes
it means avowal,[27] sometimes praise.[28] But many texts combine

---

21. J. Ratzinger, "Originalität und Überlieferung in Augustinus Begriff der 'Confessio' " in *Revue des Études Augustiniennes* 3 (1957), 375-392.
22. Cf. G. Lafont, "Le sacrifice de la Cité de Dieu. Commentaire au De Civ.
Dei, livre X, ch. 1 à VII," in *Recherches de science religieuse* 53 (1965): 177-219.
23. Ratzinger, *loc. cit.,* p. 391.
24. *Os, lingua, mens, sensus, vigor/Confessionem personent. . . .*
25. Cf. A. Blaise, *Le vocabulaire latin des principaux thèmes liturgigues* (Brépols,
1966), pp. 142-143.
26. *Et nos novi per veniam/Novum canamus canticum. . . .*
27. RB 7:44.
28. *Ibid.,* 16:4-5.

them. For accusation of faults some legislators use this verse from Psalms 105 and 107: "Give thanks to the Lord for he is good,"[29] as if to say both "acknowledge your faults to the Lord" and "praise the Lord for he is good and his love is eternal." St Benedict regards humility as a monk's habitual disposition before God, and gives another Psalm verse (75:11): "For the thoughts of man will confess to you, O Lord!"[30] Man's humility is God's glory.

St Gregory could be said to find in the word *confessio* the "most adequate expression for the complete attitude of the one who prays: admission of his own guilt and praise of God's greatness."[31] "We expiate our faults with weeping and we stand in God's presence with the words of the Psalmist, confessing his praise."[32] In this world, as St Augustine wrote, the two aspects of confession are inseparable. In the resurrection, praise alone will remain. St Gregory wrote that

> When we repent and confess our sins we enter into life by the narrow gate. And when we enter into eternal life, the very citadel of confession of praise becomes ours. It will then be no narrow gate that admits us to the joy of the eternal and everlasting banquet. . . .[33]

So, confession is linked with eschatology in its two successive stages of realization: here is our condition as sinners, there as those risen in the Lord. We are already anticipating the result, the ultimate stage, now by the one, now by the other. "Our confession of praise to God is our way of keeping with high festival a holy solemnity."[34]

Cassiodorus untiringly repeats the same idea in his *Commentary on the Psalms*. He too points to the twofold sense of *confessio*, showing how it includes both praise of God and sorrow for sin, and insisting that both connotations be kept in

29. *Ibid.*, 7:46. Likewise in the *Regula Magistri* 10:63; 14:28 ed. A. de Vogüé, in *Sources Chrétiennes* 105-106 and in the *Regula Donati* 41, PL 67:286.

30. *Ibid.*, 7:17.

31. G. Penco, "La preghiera presso il monachesimo occidentale del socolo VI" in *La preghiera . . ., op. cit.*, p. 494.

32. St Gregory the Great, *Hom. in Ev.* 1:10; PL 76:1114.

33. *Hom. in Ezechiel*, II, 4, 1; PL 76:973.

34. *Ibid.*, 11, 6,2; 1009.

mind here. "The people are to confess their sins and never to cease proclaiming the Lord's glory."[35]

The whole of this acquired tradition was to be retained in medieval patristics. Carolingian prayer books use the word "humble confession" for the prayer of the Christian accusing himself before the "great mercy" of the One who created heaven and earth.[36] Later still, Heinrich of Augsburg,[37] Bruno of Würzburg[38] and Peter Lombard[39] all use confession in the sense of repentance and praise. John of Fécamp composed an exposition on the doctrine of the Church, which was at the same time a theological confession, entitled, *Confession of Faith.* Along with all tradition previous to him he regarded theology as primarily praise, adoration, prayer, touched off by the contemplation of truth. But it is the homage of a man conscious of his sinfulness and grateful to God for pardon and help. Sorrow and admission of sin go hand in hand with gratitude: confession is a "giving of thanks."[40]

Fresh thought comes with Hervé du Bourg-Dieu, a twelfth-century monk. He describes in three words the praise offered by the Church of the Word Incarnate to the Father: *praedicatio, confessio* and *laus.* The first is an official and public proclamation of the mystery of God. It is one form of the "new canticle." *Confessio* is a more personal aspect of praise. The word suggests something individual, something intimate. It is essentially an acknowledgement, an external acknowledgement of a truth inwardly recognized and possessed: the witness of the heart breaking out in words that reveal it to others. Confession of sins, then, is admission, accusation, open self-revelation before God. . . . But confession is concerned not so much with

35. *In Ps.* 66, CC, 97, p. 582. Other texts indicated by Penco *loc. cit.,* p. 495, n. 98.

36. *Humilis confessio,* ed. A. Wilmart, *Precum libelli quattuor aevi Karolini* (Rome, 1940), pp. 21-24.

37. "*Confessio: accusativa-laudativa,*" ed. Marvin L. Colker, *Heinrici Augustensis Planctus Evae* in *Traditio* 12 (1956): 229.

38. "Confessio quasi *confacio* dicitur, sive paenitentiae, sive laus multorum ore celebrata."—*In Ps* 99; PL 142:351.

39. "Confessio gemina est: una est laudis, altera peccatorum."—*In Ps.,* IC; PL:191, 897.

40. In *Un maître de la vie spirituelle au XIe siècle* (Paris, 1946) p. 76, and *passim,* I have quoted and edited the texts.

our sins as with our love for God, our wonder in the Lord and his works—and this is a form of worship. . . ."[41] It prepares for the pardon of sins and derives from it. The new song belongs to the new man. It is a song unknown to the old man for he had not laid aside the sins of Adam. . . ."[42] In confession, then, "the love in a Christian's heart for the Lord rises to his lips and is expressed outwardly, unhindered by human consideration or human respect."[43]

Lastly, St Bernard of Clairvaux, the greatest of the twelfth-century Fathers, combines the whole thought of the Bible and early patristic tradition in many fine sentences. One sample will suffice:

> You true confessors, use every form of praise at once. Be clothed with praise as with a garment.[44] Moreover, let your inmost being praise the Lord. By the confession of sins and by the confession of praise, let your whole life confess him![45]

It is clear that St Bernard, like Scripture itself, loved to associate the idea of confession with beauty: *confessio et pulchritudo.*[46] Confession is the act of one who has refound his inner beauty, the budding of its glory to come.

CONCLUSIONS

Such, then was the traditional understanding of confession for the greater part of the Church's history. Later theology made a more precise distinction between the realities inherent in this tradition, sometimes treating them separately.[47] On

---

41. G. Oury, "Musique et Louange de Dieu d'après Hervé du Bourg-Dieu" in *Etudes grégoriennes* 8 (Solesmes, 1967): 17.

42. Hervé du Bourg-Dieu, *In Is* 42:10; PL 181:403. Other references are given by G. Oury, p. 20.

43. G. Oury, p. 19.

44. Cf. Ps 103:1, and Ps 118:18. As usual in St Bernard all this vocabulary abounds in biblical references.

45. *In Vig. Nativ.* 2:1; *S. Bernardi opera,* vol. 4 (Rome, 1966), pp. 203-204.

46. *In resurrectione* 2:10; *Ibid;* vol. 5 (Rome, 1968), p. 100. I hope to devote a special study to St Bernard's idea of *confessio.*

47. St Thomas in the *Summa theol.* II—III, q. 3, a. 1, ad lum, refers to the

the other hand, pious devotions long kept them united. For
example, the Italian penitents from the thirteenth century
on used to sing continuous hymns of praise while taking the
discipline. Even down to our own times, there are fraternities
of penitents in Latin American countries who have preserved
this combination of penance and praise—the *alabanzas*. Then,
too, confession is everywhere finding a new place in public
worship at present.

It had never disappeared from the liturgy altogether. The
West had always preserved the general confession in the Mass.
In fact, there was too much stress on it at some periods and
we find it not only at the foot of the altar but before the
Offertory too, and again before the communion. The confession before the Offertory disappeared long ago, that before
the communion a few years ago, and now there is none even
at the foot of the altar, if Mass is preceded by one of the liturgical hours. Even when it does occur, it involves only the priest.

Father Jungmann recently requested that a place be found
for it again somewhere in the Mass[48] and the same wish was
expressed at the Synod of Bishops in 1967.

The full significance of the rite should be restored, however, not simply the rite itself. Tradition fosters the interpretation and explanation of confession of sins, whether made
privately or during public worship, as bound up with the confession of praise. It is an act of adoration, a means of sharing
in the paschal mystery as a sacrifice of worship, a form of
eucharist. This fuller understanding of a sacrament which
unites the Church with the death and resurrection of Christ,
ensuring their efficacy in our souls, will lead to less emphasis
on psychological factors and superstition. Moreover, it demands the operation of faith. Christian confession is a theological reality and therefore deeper than the purely moral or
juridical. It is a gift of the Holy Spirit, a manifestation of
his action on man. It comprises both accusation of one-

three realities signified by *confessio,* which relate to three distinct virtues: the
first, *confessio fidei,* is an act of faith; the second, *confessio gratiarum et laudis*
is an act of latria (worship); the third, *confessio peccatorum* is an act of penance.

48. J. A. Jungmann SJ, "De Actu poenitentiali infra Missam inserto, conspectus
historicus" in *Ephemerides liturgicae* 70 (1966): 257-264.

self and praise of God. It requires contrition and also derives from it. Moreover, it is the source of spiritual joy and also its condition and expression. Remigius of Auxerre provides us with our conclusion in his commentary on the beginning of Psalm 105:

> *Confitemini Domino. . . . Praise the Lord and acknowledge your guilt to him, for he is good and his great love is eternal.* This is the confession of contrition since the text continues: *We have sinned, as our fathers.* But it is to be taken as the confession of praise too, for the whole text is preceded by *Alleluia.* No confession is useful, nor is it an act of piety, unless it praises God.[49]

---

49. *In Ps.* 105; PL 131:688-689.

CHAPTER VIII

REVIEW OF LIFE AND THE
CHAPTER OF FAULTS

MANY OF OUR CATHOLIC GROUPS are attaching considerable importance to "revision of life." It already has a history and literature of its own and is given a practical synthesis in a well documented book by J. Bonduelle OP.[1] The topic has been dealt with by other writers since then. There is some foundation for connecting it with the monastic "chapter of faults"—a practice which, under various forms, was also adopted by many non-monastic institutes. Like everything else, this practice needs its own *aggiornamento*. Some are of the opinion that the old custom could well draw fresh inspiration from the newer process of the review of life.

We shall treat of the chapter of faults here as part of the penance characteristic of the life of contemplatives and indeed of all religious. This should help to show the connection between the chapter of faults and the review of life.

To begin with, we need to be clear about what constitutes the review of life. For it often happens that it is regarded as an answer to all needs and a solution for all difficulties. We need a clear cut notion as to how this review of life differs from the chapter of faults and therefore how it could help to revitalize it.

---

1. *La revision de vie, Situation actuelle* (Paris: Cerf, 1964). The quotations to be given in this chapter without any other reference than the pages indicated will be borrowed from this book.

THE REAL MEANING OF THE TERMS

The expression "chapter of faults" is a monastic expression deriving from what is called the "chapter room," the place for some of the common exercises. According to tradition, a chapter of the Rule was read there every day. Capitulars, that is, those with a "voice at chapter," would meet there for discussion, voting and elections. The chapter of faults has been adopted by many religious Institutes that do not have a chapter, and in this case it applies to the meeting where the admission of negligences or infringements of rule or custom is made in common. The monastic chapter of faults, from which these others are devised, is characterized by two constituent elements:

It is a form of *self-accusation*: an act of humility on the part of a man who knows his own sinfulness, an act of penance on the part of a Christian who, in a life consecrated to God, wishes to work steadily and continuously at his own conversion.

It is a form of *fraternal correction,* providing an occasion for the exercise charity on the part of religious who live in common and recognize their common responsibility for their individual and collective spiritual good.

To understand *review of life,* we need a brief resumé of its history. It began thirty years ago in Catholic Action, or more specifically in the Catholic Action Workers' Movement. It was Cardjin's inspiration for the Young Christian Worker (J.O.C.) and was condensed into three words "see, judge, act." Later, when there were adults formed in the movement, it was the third stage—action—which gave rise to this review of life which now appears to be an important contribution which Catholic Action and especially the working world have made to the life of the Church.

Little was known about the practice at first and little study was given it, but since about 1950 many practical and, more recently, theological studies have been published on it. As is normal, the practice existed long before people formulated a theory about it. We live before we reflect about how we live.

Then a statement was made by the archbishops of two important cities: the Cardinal of Paris in his Lenten Pastoral for 1963 and the Cardinal of Brussells-Malines in a book on nuns. This latter expressed the desirability of the chapter of faults being influenced by the techniques used in review of life. This method of Catholic Action has experienced an evolution since its origin, But its constant aim has been to sift and examine. Within Catholic Action, review of life was tried by groups other than the workers' movement; young people and adults in student and farmer organizations and others. It was also tried by others outside of the Catholic Action Movement, such as missionary groups. In all these cases, the importance of the review of life varied according to circumstances. The methods used were both practical and variable, but in essentials it retained its identity and was faithful to its origins.

What is review of life? In the first place, what do the actual words mean? "Review" comes from the Latin words *revidere* or *revisere*, meaning "to see again, to come back in order to have another look, to consider, to inspect something anew." And what do we look at? Not at some fixed, immovable or lifeless object but at life, at a human experience, at some event that has occured. As it is a question of a Catholic Action group, the review is undertaken collectively. So the basic element in any definition of review of life is that it is "an interchange concerning actual fact of life among people committed to action, functioning as a group within the Church." (p. 94)

Let us now subject the content of this definition to analysis. The first point to emerge is that the practice we are considering derives from a spirituality of action and action within the specific type of group that forms a team rather than a community in the broad sense. As an assessment of activities, review is the special province of those who give themselves to the work of the apostolate, dealing with the group's involvement in this field. As a group activity it needs numbers small enough to allow for easy round-table conversation (p. 74). The word "team" is used a lot in sports today. Its Italian equivalent is *squadra,* which shows that "team" itself was originally a naval term. A common task is what unites the members of a team:

> If there is a notion of community basic to review of life it is not that of common expenditure for food, housing, or finance, such as canonists require for religious communities, but the common undertakings. It demands. a common purpose for which all pull together. The task makes the team. The life of any group calls forth some common activity and this, in turn, provides and develops incentive for review of life. Strictly speaking, this does not apply to the contemplative life. There is certainly an element of contemplation in all authentic Christian living, even in "active" life. But the thought is here determined by the meaning which traditional theology gives to "active" and "contemplative," distinguishing them as two separate ways of Christian life which primarily direct the expression of charity toward the transcendent God or toward God as present in others. The structure, scope and spiritual context of review of life restrict it to active Christian living (pp. 74-75).

Let us also remark that review of life is usually, though not always, directed by one who has the responsibility to do the preparatory work, decide the topic, direct it, safeguard it against digression and draw it to its conclusion.

The Catholic Action Group aims at affecting a specific area in Church and society, the one to which the members of the group belong. The focus of the review is not brought to bear primarily on the personal good of each of the members nor on any task of the group as a whole. In fact, review adopts and applies the view point of faith, but it must supply the occasion for developing a spiritual approach rich in content. What review is in fact seeking is the illumination of faith. Prayer is its preparation and the Gospel is the standard by which the particular situation is judged. Only a life consciously shaped on Christian principles and by the deliberate development of one's own judgment can prepare for this review. In all these respects it is an encounter with God in real events and practical situations. It helps the Christian to discern God's action in the make-up of human existence. It is also a missionary call, an invitation to encounter God in one's neighbor and to express in practical ways one's faith in God's saving will accomplished in Christ, one's hope in being able to help a brother through grace, and one's love producing a strong sense of solidarity and responsibility. The desire to act in the truth leads to self-examination concerning the harmony between action and faith—not exclusivley, or even primarily in one's personal life but from the apostolic point of view. The person involved in Catholic Action lives in the world, pursuing a secular career marked by events that are in themselves worldly. He is constantly asking himself whether he has learned how to discern God's finger in these events, how to recognize the Lord's ways, and if he has been able to alert his neighbor to God's voice.

This could be called the proto-type of review of life as conceived by Catholic Action. As it developed and spread further, its form became more varied. Its style varied with the situation it was called to meet. Groups of missionary priests, for instance, were concerned not with the secular life of a working milieu but the pastoral life in a given field of their priestly apostolate. They examined the actual situation either as it developed during a short period or a full year. But the review still had an element in "active spirituality." This gave it value but also limited its scope for it is only one of the composites of the spirituality of action.

Even within Catholic Action itself, the review does not meet every need. It must be preceded and followed by much sifting and accompanied by reflection on the Gospel. It has its dangers and difficulties and has sometimes fallen a prey to the artificial and the expedient. It has survived, however, and proved its worth. The interest roused outside its own context and particularly among religious is now readily understandable. Now to consider its possibilites in religious life, particularly with regard to the chapter of faults.

POINTS OF DIFFERENCE AND SIMILARITY

What we have just said about the chapter of faults and the review of life is enough to show that they are two distinct practices. The self-accusation which is characteristic of the first has no place in the second. "No judgement is passed on a brother's way of acting, even by the whole group, but all share their thoughts on the situation under discussion" (p. 160). The difference between the chapter of faults and the review rises from the basic purpose of each: the chapter of faults envisages the spiritual advantages of the persons concerned—both those who express humility and sorrow and those in whose presence they do so. It is meant to promote the spiritual good of the community as such: fidelity to its purpose, its service of God, the responsibilities of each of its members. But in the review, all are concentrated on a task in hand, on some definite apostolate in and for a milieu outside that of the actual review. It is not an examination of conscience, then, and does not presuppose it, comprise it or even lead to it, ordinarily. The examen is left to the individual and is made in God's presence but the review is the activity of a group oriented outwards. Only the first includes a private admission of faults.

Moreover, the review is not the exercise of fraternal correction as a form of charity described by the Lord in the Gospel according to St Matthew 18: 15-17:

> There is need for clarity on this point: the aim of the review is definitely not to convert its group of zealous members into the type of community to which the Lord says the sinful brother is to be denounced. It is not to resemble even the "one or two" to whom he wants recourse to be first made. Review fosters an atmosphere of simplicity and trust along with blunt sincerity. If accusation is made in this sort of context, it need not, perhaps, be absolutely excluded. It is generally found that such an atmosphere fosters openness with one's brothers, without any deliberate effort. It would be amiss to use the review of life for a purpose other than its own. It normally pro-

duces a righting of wrongs and amendment, but not through fraternal correction. Those who take part in the review are generally more aware than most of the duty of fraternal correction. They know how to have a word with a brother, aside. Perhaps they will look among their own members for the "one or two witnesses" mentioned by the Lord in the second case. But this need not be so. In any case, the review can never provide the context for the third suggestion—a painful one indeed. One must be categorical on this point, in spite of the misconceptions encountered here and there (p. 93).

This may seem to deny any connection between the review and the chapter of faults. There could be a double link, however, if the review really helps to give or restore life to the chapter of faults and if it offers a complement to it. To resume:

The possible advantage of the review for the chapter of faults has been dealt with in two sets of documents, deriving from the mature thought and experience of two spiritual men of our times, each speaking for the milieu in which he lived.

First, the teaching of Fr Voillaume to the Little Brothers of Jesus. In several places, he practically identifies the two practices:

We want to stress the role of the daily review of life. It requires a double effort on our part of openness toward others and of fraternal correction. The cloistered monk seeks support in monastic observances; we find it in other means offered by the life of our fraternity, and the review of life is one of them. If we want to keep our knowledge clear and our effort generous, each one of us will find that nothing can substitute for the review. This common discussion sums up the exterior expression of your fraternal life and makes it worth while. . . .

Apart from its other advantages, the review will be a steady help to you in getting to know yourself, if you practice it generously and humbly. Like all other concerted human efforts, it can be painful and prickly. We need a bit of courage to remain open to others in unaffected frankness and sincerity. And we need it again to tell a brother, quietly and without exaggeration, that we see him failing

on some particular point. Others, especially those who live with us, are quicker than we are ourselves to notice the result of an effort or, on the otherhand, the beginning of laxity, especially where our dominant defect of character is concerned. . . .
In the matter of fraternal charity, there must be no delay in pointing out the irregularities and failures that present problems to any particular brother: argumentativeness, a closed mind, stilted silence, etc. It should be one of the aims of the evening meeting to maintain this constant effort in promoting deeper fellowship among all. This will not be done without hurts and repulses. But, while they are inevitable, they must always be the starting point of deeper generosity (pp. 118-120).

The Rule will be the standard for assessing one's own fidelity and one's duty to help others in theirs:

"Anyone who wants to live the Rule must be ever sifting it. Each week, the review could bring up one point or other. Those that seem less necessary at first sight must not be put off or ignored. Always be ready to welcome the comments of your brothers on any point at all (p. 121).

From this approach, then, the review approximates to what chapter of faults should be.
The other witness indicating possible resemblance between the two practices comes from a monk, Dom Emmanuel de Miscault, Abbot of the Cistercian monastery of Timadeuc. In a remarkably clear and courageous statement, he denounced the routine, formalism and individualism endangering the monastic observance known as chapter of faults and suggested that revision might provide the remedy. He cited some historic texts, in particular a page from a Benedictine of the Congregation of St Maur, Dom Claude Martin. This seventeenth-century monk pointed out the custom of fraternal correction among the early monks. It was part of their community meetings and discussions. His point drew comment and he developed it with great humility:

With the Christian world so alert in the quest for authenticity in Gospel living and a transformation of its milieu by the Gospel spirit, the monastic world should surely find inspiration in this quest. Can it hold that its reactions, in some matters, are always characterized by utter fidelity to the line of the pure Gospel? Is it as sanctifying as it should be and could be?. . ."

It would seem that we need to draw inspiration from the means employed in Catholic Action for the transformation of its milieu if we are to effect an ever active transformation of our own. And this we are in fact bound to do, under penalty of decline. . . .

Such transformation of milieu will be planned to foster the contemplative life of monks in the best possible way. The quest must not be geared primarily to apostolic witness but to the more earnest promotion of an authentically contemplative life. It should be well understood that such promotion can be sought only in the perspective of the apostolic life described in the Acts of the Apostles, the evangelical life and the spirit of the Beatitudes (pp. 151, 153).

THE LESSONS OF EXPERIENCE

What conclusion is to be drawn from the points of difference and similarity between the review and the chapter of faults? What answer have we to the problem of their relationship? The facts have already spoken for themselves, and we sum this up in two suggestions.

Since the review of life derives from lived experience, *the doctrine basic to it may well foster renewal of the chapter of faults.*

It concentrates on the Gospel as the standard according to which self-accusation is made and mutual correction given. Certainly the goal of the Rule is to foster the fidelity of religious to the Gospel but there is always the danger of priority being given to observances that are no more than set ways of doing things and are sometimes more exterior than interior. Accusations are made on the basis of failures committed against observances. Religious run the risk of attaching less importance to the Christian life than to its forms and less importance to the essential commitment of the religious state than to the details of daily routine. There is real need for examination, accusation and correction in the matter of fidelity to the deep challenge of the Gospel, to the call which the Lord is making to each member of a community and to a group as a whole: these matters constitute the very heart of existence. The chapter of faults remains or becomes a fully personal activity when practiced in full realization of the extent of its obligation, with complete sincerity and in the presence of the One who dwells in all hearts and is the sole witness of their inner content. "We glory in the witness of our conscience." We have seen that the review of life constitutes part of a meeting devoted to Gospel reflection and carried on in a spirit of prayer. The chapter of faults needs the same recollected approach, it is not a ceremony or an exterior rite—still less a solemn one: it must be an act of religion.

The review can become the complement of the chapter of faults. Though not to be confused with it, the revision can be added to it with a different frequency and in relation to other matters. Apart from the observance of the Rule and the internal life of communities, there are areas of relationship between communities and the world where communities exercise or should exercise influence or apostolic and missionary activity on the secular situation and the surrounding social milieu. It would be natural for communities to "review" their conduct in all these spheres. This is clearly indicated in regard to the contemplative monasteries themselves:

> Our abbeys are progressively less able to avoid what *Mater et Magistra* calls socialization. Life within a closed economy is progressively less possible for them and abbeys find themselves exercising pastoral activities. Complete isolation is rarely possible in contemporary life and the whole field of contact with the outside world assumes the character of Christian contact with worldly people or with Christians confronting the world or with non-Christians.
> We ask ourselves how the review of life becomes necessary through the extent of direct and indirect contact with the world. Is the cenobitic life possible nowadays without some concern for those whom we call neighbors? Can we opt for Gospel living and at the same time remain impervious to the question of its transparence or non-transpar-

ence to the modern mind? Can we claim a given monastic
tradition as our inheritance without enquiring whether
our contemporaries read in it a sign of the Beatitudes, or
a countersign? (p. 145)

Active religious institutes have very good reason for questioning the relation between the occupations to which they are
devoted and the structures, the mental outlook and the en-
vironmental evolutions amid which their apostolate is exercised
and their life lived. There may be occasional or regular meetings to consider these topics, involving either the entire community or else commissions or other groups set up to deal
with different matters. The aim of the review of life will be
quite different. Review of life and the chapter of faults have a
different goal and different subject matter. Review is not
identical with the chapter of faults but supplements it.

To conclude we quote from a document of considerable
interest. On the one hand it is perfectly traditional, preserving
the essential doctrine of monasticism; and on the other, quite
new, giving inspiration to various realizations in the Foucauld's
tradition. This document is the Rule of life published in 1966
and entitled *Au coeur même de l'Église. Une recherche de vie
monastique: les Frères de la Vierge des pauvres.*[2] The
expression chapter of faults does not occur, but in the chapter
on "Fraternal Exchange" gives a description of the different
forms this may assume; "meetings," which are a time for
formation and religious instruction; "openness," "review of
life," "discussions," "fraternal correction." The last-mentioned
is treated apart since it is done in private. The chapter of
faults is treated as "fraternal openness." It takes place at the
beginning of Compline and comprises examination and accusation. It is distinct from the review, which bears on the life of
the fraternity and fidelity to the spirit and duties of the vocation. One would really need to give examples from the lengthy
and beautiful sections devoted to interior attitudes which the
brothers should have during this exercise and to its subject-
matter and limitations.

2. (Paris: Desclée de Brouwer, 1966). See especially pp. 166-179.

Let it suffice to draw attention to this document. It gives coordination and order to the various expressions of community life and unifies them by the spirit in which they are performed. This spirit is expressed in passages like the following:

> Fraternal openness must always remain natural and spontaneous. Before you open your heart to a brother, recollect that it is Jesus to whom you speak, Jesus to whom you reveal your faults; it is Jesus with whom you share your difficulties, Jesus who is present in person in the midst of them. You must believe this with your whole heart, and sometimes it will be hard.
>
> Fraternal openness is, above all, a mystery of faith. . . . You must believe in the love that each brother has for all the others, and that the Lord has called them all to him, that they may work together in fellowship, in his presence. . . . In this way, the review of life will bear fruit and loving fidelity will be strengthened within the brotherhood.

CHAPTER IX

CONTEMPLATIVE AFRICA[1]

O UR TOPIC INVOLVES AN EXAMINATION of
fidelity to one of the teachings of Vatican II, expressed in the *Decree on the Missionary Activity of the
Church.* Chapter Two (no. 18) prescribes that the religious
life in its various forms should constitute part of the Church's
growth in countries not yet fully evangelized. The Council
lays down a principle of adaptation which applies to all forms
of religious Life:

> Religious institutes which labor for the spread of the
> Church, profoundly impregnated with the mysteries of
> holiness which are the glory of the religious tradition of
> the Church must endeavor to express them and transmit
> them according to the genius and character of each nation.
> They must examine how their ascetic and contemplative
> traditions, the germs of which have sometimes been spread
> by God in ancient civilizations before the preaching of
> the Gospel, can be assumed into religious life.

Then the Council speaks in detail about one particular form of religious life:

> Worthy of special mention are the various initiatives de-
> signed to make contemplative life take root. Some insti-
> tutes, preserving the essential elements of the monastic
> institution, will labor to implant the very rich tradition
> of their order; others will return to the simplest forms of

1. This is developed from an article appearing in *Vivante Afrique* 256 (May-June,
1968): 1-4.

early monasticism, but all must seek an authentic adaptation to local conditions. The contemplative life belongs to the full development of the presence of the Church, and must be implanted everywhere in the young Churches.

Further on, in Chapter 4 (no. 40), the same *Decree* states:

Institutes of contemplative life, by their prayers, their works of penance and their sufferings, are of great importance in the conversion of souls, since it is God who answers our prayers by sending workers into his harvest (cf. Mt 9:38), opens the hearts of non-Christians to listen to the Gospel (cf. Acts 16:14), and makes the word of salvation fruitful in their hearts (cf. 1 Cor 3:7). These institutes are invited to found houses in mission countries, as some have already done, so that living their life in a manner authentically adapted to the religious traditions of the people, they may give to non Christians a splendid witness of the majesty and love of God and of union in Christ.

A WORD ON HISTORY

Monks and nuns had anticipated the Church's teaching on this point, especially during the last thirty years, and even more during the last fifteen or so. At present there are monasteries in Africa, Madagascar, Asia and Martinique; and every year sees more foundations and fresh preparations. Among the African monasteries, special mention is due to the Priory of Saint Maur at Hanga in Tanzania. Even at this stage, its prior and community are fully African, and their way of life is expressed in special statutes approved by the Congregation for Religious. They follow the Benedictine life adapted to Africa. Having already written several articles relating to African monasticism,[2] we give here just a brief outline of its principal characteristics.

History is built on geography. From an atlas of Church history with a map showing the origin and development of

---

2. See *Chances de la spiritualité occidentale,* pp. 87-124 and *Aspects du Monachisme,* pp. 323-342.

monasticism in the early centuries of Christianity, we find that Africa and especially Egypt provide the oldest and most numerous examples of monks living alone and living in common, whose life was recognized by the Church. St Antony was to gain the approval of a bishop eager to foster this kind of life. He withdrew into the desert of Tahennesei and returned to Alexandria only once. This was to care for the sick during an epidemic—a fact which shows, from the very outset, that solitude does not dispense the monk from charity. Monasticism soon spread throughout the East, north to Asia Minor, south to Ethiopa, west to what the Romans called Africa and Mauritania and modern Tunisia, the birthplace of St Augustine who did so much for monks. During this same period, the entire West was giving birth to monks who drew inspiration from the example of that great African, St Antony. Monasticism spread through Europe, and later, through America. It is still very much alive in Egypt and Ethiopia and is now coming back from the West to the continent that cradled it: northern and Negro Africa.

A modern map of monastic Africa would show about fifty communities of monks and nuns of the Benedictine and Cistercian Orders, covering almost the whole span of the continent. Then there are numerous communities of Carmelites, Poor Clares, Redemptoristines and contemplatives of other observances, which are also part of the monastic phenomenon.[3] Monastic life has strong roots in African soil. In such vast country there is room for many more foundations. The future is wide open and already full of promise. What is needed now is encouragement to foster this growth, direction for the whole movement, organization for what is already in existence.

The A. I. M. (*Aide à l'Implantation Monastique*) was founded to further this goal. The Secretariat is centered with the Benedictines of Vanves and its activities cover Asia and Latin America as well as Africa where it bore its first fruits. After a great deal of preparatory work through enquiries and questionnaires, a meeting of monastic superiors was held at Bouaké in 1964. It was followed up by regional meetings in different

3. A table of statistics is to be found in *Vivante Afrique, loc. cit.*, pp. 28-29.

parts of the continent and then by a Congress in Rome in 1966, which established the African Conference of Monastic Superiors. African monasticism is thus taking shape. What then are its characteristics?

THE SITUATION AND ROLE IN THE MISSIONS

The *Decree on the Missionary Activity of the Church* has indicated that contemplative life should be implanted in the young churches and adapted to the condition and traditions of each country. It is not a matter of providing monks and nuns with missionary or pastoral work for which they have neither the vocation nor formation, but rather of introducing the full life of the Church, complementing its apostolate with contemplative prayer. In this way, Christian men and women everywhere will have the chance to live this kind of life without being deprived of their own cultural values.

Even in 1964 this conviction was clear at the meeting at Bouaké. The same principle was authoratively confirmed by Paul VI in an audience for those participating in the Congress at Rome in 1966. Turning toward a group of them, with obvious enthusiasm he expressed his pleasure:

> And here is another missionary group—the superiors of the African Benedictine monasteries—monk and nuns.
> There is something here for all of us to notice. Mainly, of course, because it is something involving Africa which is, so to speak, the very heart of the Church's missionary hopes, concern and longing. Africa has certainly borne good fruit, but she is also a continent in desperate need.
> The interesting thing in this case is that these monks and nuns are apostles. Now this may seem like a contradiction in terms. Is it not true that the monk is concerned with himself rather than with others? Is he not walled up in his cloister, with no concern for the world about him? But here we have evidence of just the opposite.
> History tells us that Europe was evangelized for the most part by monks, especially by Benedictines. From their cloisters they spread abroad the Christian life, the word of the Lord and the sacraments. They labored for the spiritual

growth of their neighbors—non-Christian, pagan and even barbarian. The missionary activity of Benedictines is specific to them and emanates from the monasteries themselves; each house is a spiritual center. In each you will find the divine office, the chant, the liturgy, silence, community, the alternation of manual with spiritual work, the *Ora et labora,* as St Benedict taught. This is a grand ideal. Other missionaries go about, journeying across mountains and valleys. The Benedictine approach is very different, but it is praised by history, blessed by the Church and full of promise.

We grant a very special blessing, then, to these monks and nuns, to those who help them and to those helped by them.

You have shown no small courage in consecrating your abbeys, priories and communities to this apostolate. Match this courage with confidence in St Benedict and St Scholastica, and in your tradition. Enter into it fully. Those of you who run schools and dispensaries will understand that your apostolate comprises word and work. But for all of you, without exception, your deepest apostolate derives from the spiritual energy emanating from the Benedictine community as from a glowing source of faith and love.

What the Holy Father said to these Benedictines is clearly applicable to all forms of monastic life, for all share the same tasks, the same responsibility, the same hope, and their pluralism of form is evidence of the richness of the Church.

RETURN TO THE SOURCES AND RADIATION OF INFLUENCE

Twice in his address, the Pope spoke of "radiation." This reminds one of the heart as the source of light and energy. There are two African foundations at Katanga and Dakomey, expressing this notion in their very name: Our Lady of the Sources and St Benedict of the Sources. But all the others spring from the sources too. It is significant, perhaps, that monasteries are most numerous in the region of the Great Lakes, source of the two great trans-African rivers, the Nile and the Congo, linking Africa with the Mediterranean world and the Atlantic. Monasticism is returning to its sources—yes, and especially to its sources in the African soul. At the Congress in Rome, Father E. M'veng, a Jesuit from the Cameroons, had this to say:

> The monastic vocation must express a response not only to the needs of individuals in the religious life, but to those of the Church in different countries and also to the basic issues determining the destiny of our peoples, in so far as that destiny has a radically religious dimension. Monasticism must fulfill the contemplative potential of Africa's sons within her ecclesial communities, so that the universal Church may be brought to full spiritual stature.
>
> Negro-African civilization is essentially religious. It was fostered at such centers of spirituality as fetish-monasteries, initiation brotherhoods enters and Contemporary Africa is a place of change. Inner conversion is in process and the cults of former days are being abandoned. her spiritual centers? Where will African art, music, dance, architecture and dress seek their inspiration and symbolism while preserving their authentic Negro African spirit. It may be that Africa will look to the monastic life to recharge her spiritual potential today and tomorrow.

Monasticism is ancient, the oldest form of religious life in the Church, and by that fact sends us back to her sources: to the Bible, the Church Fathers, especially those of the East, and the Desert Fathers. Many passages in the Old and New Testaments assume new meaning when seen against their African context, as we know from the western monks who are sent there. Moreover, African monks and nuns on their own initiative are now rediscovering the customs, dispositions and forms of prayer which came naturally to the first monks in this same continent: Africa's modern monasticism is guiding the older Western monasticism back to its living sources. This is a point of ecumenical significance.[4]

It is sometimes said that monasteries are not wanted in

4. That is what I have tried to show in a sutdy entitled "Le monachisme africain d'aujourd'hui, et le monachisme antique" in *Irénikon* 38 (1965): 97-103, reprinted in *Chances de la spiritualité*, pp. 97-120.

Africa because the need is for development, whereas "monasticism is based on contempt for the world." One only needs to see the actual situation, in order to evaluate these childish slogans. The fact is that wherever there is a monastery there is a school, dispensary, sometimes a village hospital, land development, even co-operative ventures and various types of cultivation. Paul VI alluded to the works. Although monks do not generally become directly involved, they foster them in every possible way. The monastery becomes the living heart of a whole population. In many places the people even move, so as to come and live close to the men of prayer and work. Sometimes if the community itself moves, it is followed by the whole settlement in its vicinity. The Benedictine community of Hanga in Tanzania provides one example of this type of apostolate, and of the attachment of Christians and others to the monks as their friends. The Liturgy in particular is an area where monks can carry out an apostolate for which their primary occupation of prayer prepares them.

But we must face the fact that African monasticism is still in its infancy. It is unpretentious and should preserve its simple spirit. It is far from presenting a successful and irreproachable image. In taking its first steps, it is groping and hesitant. Among the many difficulties to be faced some derive from personal frailties—poor health, human limitations, inevitable failures—and some come from God: this can be disconcerting as when a young African superior, full of hope for his community, is carried off in a matter of days by some mysterious illness and then another is killed in a car accident. Other examples could be given. The important thing is not to lose heart, but sustain the effort. "In the heart of the Church," said Paul VI, October 13, 1965, "is born a reawakening, along with restlessness, concern and hope. These stir her whole being, deepen her self-awareness, prompt her self-questioning, rouse her to creative thinking, and to the initiation of new experiments in the practical order." Monasticism has its place in this great work, and is fully devoted to it. It is not achieving success, or even looking for success. Patience is its only true foundation. Monasticism is only one means by which the mystery of the death and resurrection of Jesus Christ are made present in the world, in humility and sometimes in humiliation.

A recent issue of *Vivante Afrique* was devoted to monasticism.[5] It was the outcome of a large documentary dossier of which only a small part could be published, but this small part is revealing. A few extracts will suffice here.

THE CONTEMPLATIVE LIFE OF THE AFRICANS

The Superior of the priory of Saint Maur at Hanga in Tanzania, has spoken on behalf of his own community and many others. He brings out particularly well that the African has "his own" contemplation and must have his own "liturgy":

> From the outset, the most remarkable tendency I have noticed among us is that all, both priests and non-priests alike, are prayer-monks. To our African mind it is essential for a monk or religious to be a man of prayer . . . so we have tried to find this ideal among our European confrères; but it is especially to the Bible and Tradition that we have recourse. . . . Contemplation, as depicted by learned men in books and conferences, certainly seems exalted, attractive and feasible. But in practice it seems impossible to ask of Africans. I have even been tempted to believe that these learned people are passing on to us what they have heard rather than what they have experienced themselves . . . my trouble in understanding may derive from the fact that it is difficult to describe in words. Perhaps it comes from my own ignorance. Or perhaps there is a difference between European and African mentality. You even wonder whether an African can really become a contemplative without some special intervention on the part of providence. . . . We are told that our life

5. This appeared in May-June 1968 (n. 256) under the title *L'Afrique contemplative.* It is surprising that the Missionaries, White Fathers and White Sisters who have published this, have not hesitated to use the term "contemplative life" from the cover right on through.

is active, not contemplative, but to my mind if this is true it is something new and results from foreign influence: industrial, artificial, rationalist, materialistic, anthropocentric. The fact remains that in spite of this influence many Africans are capable of contemplation and meditation.

Christian ceremonies would be acceptable if they were integrated with Bantu gestures. Unfortunately, very many Africans, finding no satisfaction whatever in the present form of the Christian liturgy, are returning to the pagan ceremonies that they can understand. Others are taking part in both Christian liturgy and in pagan ceremonies. Foreign missionaries have done a great deal in an effort to make the Mass more attractive for the Tanzanians, but without success. The principles of Vatican II are certainly excellent in themselves, but they are generally applied according to European mentality, standards and temperament without regard for the African frame of mind. There is much to be done in our region then, to make Africans feel at home in the Christian liturgy, and derive the spiritual support they crave. In this long-range task, the African monks of Hanga will strive with might and main to share. Finally, the word "work" may comprise every type of work compatible with monastic life. We are trying to combine modern European methods with whatever is viable in our approach. When there is need, we leave off all private occupations so as to take part in a common work, as is our custom.

TOWARD AN AFRICAN MONASTICISM

Someone closely connected with the development of a monastery in Katanga has expressed the opinion that "the introduction of a European way of life and customs into a world that remains Bantu to the marrow even while evolving" causes difficulties. The Superior of a recent foundation at Congo Kinshasha expresses the following opinion:

African monasticism must be freed from Western forms which have no justification here. Existing monastic Orders will fulfill the function of moulding the new African monasticism, but no more. This demands sacrifice but it is the only way. Efficacious help from Eastern monasticism

seems absolutely necessary to us: the East is psychological-
ly closer to Africa and has remained more faithful to
early monasticism. . . . which in fact was African! And in
this Eastern monasticism I see Ethiopia foremost. I am
profoundly convinced that it is a duty of the Church to
organize systematic relations with Ethiopian Christianity
which is more African than others and has preserved a
monasticism that is very much alive.

If Africanization is necessary, it must not be to the det-
riment of Africans; African monasticism must not become
synonymous with a "watered down monasticism it must
be authentic." General monastic tradition is a heritage
"of the Church," even if the agents who actually trans-
mit it to the Africans are Westerners. Whence arises, for
example, the principle of the unique paternity of the
superior (which Paul VI recalled recently when addressing
Africa), the principle of "the clan of God" . . .

"The future of monasticism lies in Africa," as someone
has accurately assessed. The African soul is monastic by
nature. All that is needed is to Christianize her basic categories. This will need time, clear vision and self denial, but
in the end African monasticism will make its specific contribution to the patrimony of the universal Church. We have
no doubt about this.

LITURGY

In this domain let us cite the example of the fraternity of The
Virgin of the Poor, first near the Congo-Nile, and later at Lake
Kivu, acting under the advice of Bishop Bigurumwami, of
Nyondo.

On our arrival at Rwanda in 1958, we found that religious
music contained only about a dozen songs whose words
and music were truly Rwandic. As well as these there were
a number of ballads more sentimental than biblical, a few
functional, liturgical chants, no Psalms. Since then the
chants for the liturgy of the word and the Eucharist have
greatly increased. We have been experimenting with most
of these. . . .

To accompany the chant, our Bishop has encouraged the
use of the drum, the eightstringed harp and a small Rwandic "violin." A good number of Psalms like the great Hal-

lel, the Psalms of praise and acclamation were composed with the idea of rhythmic accompaniment by drums or hand-clapping. In the chapel we have the small drum for rhythm on one side and the deep booming one on the other. The minor elevation brings a long pause of acclamation and the roll of drums; the same applies to the doxology at the beginning of the Office. And each time a Psalm indicates hand-clapping or harp-accompaniment, this is carried out literally. In Advent and Lent accompaniments are suppressed. For feast days, on the other hand, we sing the Office and Mass in polyphany.

Everyone knows that the Latin rite is very reserved in comparison with the Eastern rites. To express his praise of God the African needs a medium more animated, more true to life. How is Rwanda to do this? There were hardly any ritual gestures in local tradition. The pagans had no liturgy, properly so called, to honor. This gap must be filled from the simple current gestures of ordinary life, since they express the culture and mentality of the country. Another source of inspiration for us is the Bible and the Eastern liturgies. Christians all the world over naturally want to use not only the words, but the very gestures of our Savior in their prayer. Let us beware of any false shyness preventing us! This carries particular weight in Africa, where the person expresses himself in all his original simplicity. . . . These biblical gestures have been preserved in most of the Eastern rites—even Islam has borrowed from them.

NUNS

Many contemplative nuns are realizing their ideal of contemplative life in community; the following comment comes from the Abbess of Malawi:

An African monastery must be marked by originality. The African cannot "fulfill" himself humanly or spiritually except in a group, and he must be fully free to be himself. We do not see our nuns losing their personality, but without the group, they would lack the source of life. The group gives the lifeblood, and vitality wells up in joyful expression; the person then grows to maturity. . . .

Within the monastery enclosure, there are always the ordinary tasks that are familiar to African women, and these please the nuns most of all. They go off happily with their hoe in hand to break up the soil and do the planting. They are less impressed than Europeans by the budding of a flower, or the light of an insect, but they are in deeper communion with the earth, the mystery of its fecundity, and the rhythm of the seasons. . . .
All this shows also in their outstanding gift for musical harmony and improvisation. Psalmody is not the best vehicle for their religious spontaneity, their cry for God's help, or their praise. Rather it is in the richest and most natural forms of polyphony that the inspiration of each one is sustained and heightened by that of the group. The Roman liturgy is both too bare and too rigid for them. The African needs to be left free to sing his own Magnificat at Vespers, and to dance it according to the mood of the day, if praise is to express the rhythm of his soul. By Africa's christianity, and by Africa's contemplative life, these values of communion will be given fresh life in the Church. It is a communion vital to nature and to the world, a communion in mystery with the reciprocal influences of grace more deeply understood and actualized in the Church itself. A communion in brotherhood flowing from natural and supernatural intuition. A communion such as this will send up to God a praise more worthy of the new heaven and the new earth, where all will be harmony in love and perfect communion in the Lord Jesus.

The Carmelites of Zaza in Rwanda are also facing the problems which confront them:

Our neighbors were living in huts—and these were not made of bricks (which is a sign of wealth and security in this region) so we were no longer happy in our "security". . . . We decided to transfer and to transform our monastery. We thought it was up to us to live like our neighbors, working, using local material, doing whatever they could do, Certainly we must be Carmelites first and foremost—souls of prayer and solitude; but also, Carmelites of Rwanda, women responsible for their country and its Christian evolution, women who want to be visible signs for the simple and the lowly. . . .

Following the example of Teresa of Avila, her African daughters scoured the dumps, and in no time their practical sense and natural talents combined to design modest little houses all constructed from local material. . . It is with unfeigned pride that the people discover much that it beautiful in what they have. They are not surprised to find that ordinary things gain new value in the service of the Lord.

At almost any hour of the day, there are nuns in the Church; the passing Christian can see and hear them at prayer. They may be silently recollected in an attitude of adoration, of sitting on their little mats in familiar intercourse with the Lord. Or they may be expressing themselves in the rhythmic chant of the Psalms, accompanied by a strong drum beat, the soft flute or the single tone "muduli." They use expressive gestures also; for example both hands outstretched, as if to give or receive—this is used as an aid when saying the Our Father and is a customary gesture in the country—or a profound bow accompanied by hand-clapping, a mark of great respect, replaces the genuflection.

If Carmel is to be a center of intense life in Africa, it must grow from the inner values of the people. The Africanization of structures is only the beginning. It is an indispensable break-through, but inadequate. Moreover, we are now dealing with irrevocable commitment. . . . Carmel is showing the Rwandees an aspect of Christianity they can easily grasp. The fact that there is no apostolic activity poses a question for some. The contemplative seems to be a sign of that other world which we are taught is real and to which every man is heading, even if he does not know it: we mean the world of the divine.

CHAPTER X

PROBLEMS OF CHRISTIAN MONASTICISM
IN ASIA[1]

CAN WE SPEAK OF "ASIAN MONASTICISM" as if this word "Asian" designated one single reality, when we are actually referring to a vast continent with numerous islands and archipelagoes? We need to consider monasticism in each of the countries which make up Asia and provide a rich variety. There are elements common to all: some deriving from nature, others from history. Through creation, and human traditions. God has worked at fashioning these countries and these peoples. In the words of Vatican II he had scattered seeds of truth and holiness even before the Church preached the Gospel in these places. We must try to discern these various elements, explaining them where we can with examples borrowed from different countries. We can offer only the general and superficial impressions which we have gathered in only five countries. The one justification for this chapter is that, to my knowledge, nothing else is available on the subject at present, and so nothing more comprehensive.

Our purpose here is only to state the "problems" and to suggest the causes, or at least some of them, without offering solutions. For an enquiry like this, objectivity is absolutely essential. Admiration for the authentic goodness we discover here and gratitude for the warmth and friendship we encountered must not restrict our freedom in expressing the problems and pointing out the responsibilities that derive from

1. *Collectania Cisterciensia* 30 (1968): 15-52; *Parole et mission* (1968): 437-465 (abridged version).

them. There could be a temptation to compare Asia with Africa because monastic implantation is recent in both countries and seems to have assumed the same forms. But it would be a shame to do this. It would show that monasticism is being considered in these two very different parts of the world as the same European product which has been transported to other places and that it can be assessed by comparison with its place of origin and according to the stage of parallel growth in different countries. It is, without doubt, hard to avoid this kind of transplantation at first. What is needed is the gradual creation of an autochthonous monasticism blending the rhythm of the eternal God with that of each people. It will be determined by two elements which are specific to Asia. We mentioned these above, and we return to them now.

NATURE AND ANCIENT RELIGION

Climate should be considered first among the elements deriving from nature. It always affects the physique and mentality of a people, influencing the whole man and revealing itself in his sense of time and in the rhythm of his work. There is a rich variety among the races, within a certain unity, if one compares them as a whole with the peoples of Africa, Oceania, Western Europe and its extension in America, and with America before Columbus. This fact of itself cannot but produce psychological variety.

Almost everywhere the basic food is still rice, in spite of the import of other foods from abroad. The demands of rice culture continue to determine man's rhythm of life and method of work. When men employ the same method for thousands of years for planting, harvesting, grinding, preparing and eating rice and, without doubt, for assimilating it, they are bound surely to have some characteristics in common. There is a "rice civilization," just as we speak of a "bread and wine" civilization for the Mediterranean basin. Some countries have terraced rice fields and the rice terraces are said to go back four thousand years. These countries are truly masterpieces of irrigation, land and water utilization, and agricultural planning. The "eulogy of rice" is still a traditional thing in Philippine literature, for example, and out in the country harvest festivals are kept with their fertility and fecundity rites. The ritual death of certain persons is followed by ceremonies symbolic of the soil's new birth. The "rice-dance" is part of the folk law of many places. Among the Montagnardes in Vietnam, the chief gesture of hospitality consists in inviting the stranger to "drink from the jar" of fermented-rice beer. This wonderful food which is God's gift to so many peoples certainly explains something of what they are and merits respect. Westerners cannot be said to have understood this always.

As chief among the characteristics coming to these people from God through history, we must rank their ancient religions. It is not easy to characterize them in a single word, for some have matured and in this sense are not "primitive." These religions are sometimes found in their pure state among the natives of the country in the minority groups that have been pushed back to high mountainous country. They left behind traces of their art. For example in Indonesia we find magic rods and masks expressing joy and humor, sometimes with exquisite decorations in gold or silver webbing.[2] These primitive peoples present a problem to missiology and monastic implantation. We must return to this further on. Here we need only indicate this as an ethnological and historical fact in these religions. It has its influence on the Christian reality for there are in many places traces of these ancient religions intermingled with Christianity. There is nothing surprising about this: the same sort of thing has happened in many parts of Europe.

In Manila they have a saying that: "The Spanish have made the Philippines Christian, but the Filipinos have made Christianity Filipino." Sometimes this results in a strange mixture of rites and customs, deriving from different religious traditions, but surely this is not so strange after all. The Christian church did the same thing when it took root in Rome, to mention just one other example. Our liturgy is marked, and even in a way hampered, by what has clung to it from earlier

2. To quote only one example, that of Indonesia see: *Indonesische Kunstnijverheid Platen-Atlas,* met inleiding van Pr. T. J. Bezemer, ed. J. M. Mentenhoff (Amsterdam, s. d.).

religions no longer significant for us. There are customs and costumes, feast and sacred dances from the early tribal period. These are still used to mark the anniversary of events in the country's pre-Christian history which have now been incorporated into the Christian calendar. This explains some of the funeral customs, especially the rites for November 2nd, when the whole night is spent at the cemetery, picnicking and playing mah-jong, each family with its own transistor. There are rhythmic liturgical dances accompanied by hand clapping. Even the statues, of St Martha or some other saint, are made to dance by the way the shrine is carried along. On certain days in Manila the traffic is disrupted by the crowd, coming by jeep or any other means, for the novena to the saint invoked as "Patron of Hopeless Cases." One must sometimes realize, with good humor, that all this has no connection with salvation. . . . In a "barrio" church, I have counted on the altar or in the sanctuary five statues of the Sacred Heart and six of the Madonna. Can there be any certainty that those who come along to venerate them, one by one, realize that they all represent the same Savior, Jesus, and the same Virgin Mary?

In countries where Christianity has not penetrated as deeply as in the Philippines it is easier to see both the resemblance and the distinction among the different altars found in the center of the entrance porch in each house. They are visible from the street. For the shrine of their ancestors, Catholics substitute one in honor of the saints or of Our Lord.

One day when out in the country, I entered a small non-Christian sanctuary. The picturesquely attired leaders of the local community were celebrating a thanksgiving service for the cure of a child who was represented by a pretty doll made especially for the occasion. The altars were covered with offerings of rice, salt, spices and bananas. Musicians accompanied the singing on native instruments.

These examples focus attention on one facet of the situation which Christianity and Christian monasticism have to face in Asia.

The cult of death and of the dead holds an important place

in the life of the Asiatic peoples. In one place I saw a massive coffin which a villager had gone to great expense to prepare for himself. And I have heard it said that the best gift children can offer their father for his birthday is a monumental coffin.

But apart from the archaic religions, Asia has others that are connected with the cultures that have evolved. These are extremely civilized and refined, and have deeper roots in antiquity than our Western civilization has. This fact constitutes the most important part of the monastic problem, and differentiates it from this problem in all other continents where the Church has spread. Here, for three thousand five hundred years and more before modern Christian monasticism was implanted, another type of monasticism existed, bound up with other religions and constituting part of their life. This monasticism is still flourishing.

There is a question to be asked, and we would do well to concentrate on it: Has Christian monasticism anything to learn from this ancient Asiatic monasticism, and has it anything to give the older form? The Second Vatican Council expressed this problem explicitly. In the *Decree on the Missionary Activity of the Church,* it asked those institutes that might be considering the foundation of religious life in mission lands "to assess carefully how these ascetic and contemplative traditions, seeds planted by God in ancient civilizations sometimes before the preaching of the Gospel, can be utilized for Christian religious life." We need to remind ourselves that Asia has her own specific spiritual disciplines and that Christian monasticism must take them into consideration.[3]

HINDUISM AND BUDDHISM

The first of these religious disciplines to be considered is Hinduism. Someone has remarked that it is difficult to speak of this complex reality in the singular since it really consists of various traditions—doctrinal and devotional, recent and remote. "All schools of philosophy in India have been founded

3. See the recent survey in B. Griffiths, "Hinduism" in *The Catholic Encyclopedia* (New York, 1967), 4: 1123-1136.

by saints or seers: all their teachings are based on deep spiritual experience of God, or the ultimate reality.[4] We cannot here attempt even an outline of Hindu monastic history. Father Francis Mahieu has given a masterly account of the early Vedic and Dravidian religions between 1500 and 800 BC; the confluence of these different currents and finally the great epics of Ramayana, which exemplified an ideal of ascetical life, frequently structured in a way similar to monasticism. What is written of the hermitages of those times is reminiscent of early Egyptian monasticism.[5]

With the Upanishads, about the year 700, monasticism received a strong impulse from the Brahmins, a professional religious caste. There soon developed an itinerant and mendicant monasticism, whose representatives witnessed to the instability and wretchedness of this present life. They thirst for knowledge of God and union with him in the immortality of the next world and, even in the present, by a joyful liberty of spirit in regard to worldly advantage. With the Baghavadgita there is new stress on renunciation, solitude, meditation, compassion and tranquillity of heart. Finally the Code of Manu set the life-style of the gurus, saddhus and other monks and of the ashrams or communities in relation to the different states of religious life and the different stages in each.

Buddhism seems to be an extreme example of what may be called "the monastic phenomenon" in a very advanced non-Christian religion.[6] It was probably about the sixth century BC in the Himalayas that Prince Siddharta Gautama renounced

4. John Moffitt, "A Christian Approach to Hindu Beliefs" in *Theological Studies* 27 (1967): 58-78; M. Dhavamony SJ, "The Religious Quest of Hinduism" in *Studia Missionalia* 15 (1966): 65-82.

5. On the whole history of monachism in India, besides the article of F. Mahieu, "Monasticism in India" in *The Clergy Monthly Supplement* (June-July, 1964), pp. 45-60, now translated into French under the title "La monachisme en Inde" in *Collectanea Cisterciensia* 29 (1967): 164-178, there appeared quite recently the excellent article on history and spirituality by P. J. Lopez Gay SJ, "El monacato budista" in *Boletin de la Asociacion Espanola de Orientalistas* 3 (1967): 93-118, with a select bibliography, p. 119. Sukumar Dutt, *Buddhist Monks and Monasteries of India* (London, 1962).

6. A. S. Rosso, "Buddhism" with bibliography in *The New Catholic Encyclopedia*, 2: 847-857.

his power in order to lead a monastic life. Being enlightened,
he received the name of Buddha, or "the brightened one."
The way of salvation inaugurated by him, monastic in character, was to conquer the whole of Asia. The sangha is an
order or community whose members are separated from the
world, cut off from relationship with it, wherein during a
period of probation, which may last for ten years, one is
formed by a master. Then the symbol of the monastic state
is received, the begging bowl which to this day is carried by
many Bonzas. A kind of penal code comprising 250 articles
furnishes material for a periodical "chapter of faults." A prom-
inent characteristic of this kind of monasticism is a certain
benevolence expressing itself in respect for the life of all
creatures, in restraint from killing animals and in involvement
in works of charity comparable with those which have always
been practiced in Christian monasteries. The monks seek and
find that interior peace and joy which one sees reflected in
the faces of so many of them. They devote themselves to
meditation,—the symbol of which, the figure of the seated,
cross-legged Buddha, holds so familiar a place in the art of
many countries. It is this figure one sees in a good proportion
of the works of art on exhibition in the national museum of
Phom-Penh, Cambodia, as in that of the Art Kmer in Vietnam or at Djakarta in Indonesia. In this last country among
the ruins of the temple of Barabudur, which was built some-
time after the end of the eighth century, there are no less than
504 statues of the Buddha, generally seated on the lotus which
is a symbol of purity, one or other of his favorite attitudes,
and above all, wrapped in meditation. Twenty kilometers from
Barabudur there is a Cistercian monastery. Remembering the
important place meditation holds in Christian monasticism
it is hard to resist the temptation of making a comparison.[7]

In our day, the influence of Hindu monasticism was demon-
strated by the fact that Gandhi, after having lived as a monk

7. While in a Christian Monastery in Asia reading G. Constant Lounnsbery,
La méditation bouddhique, (Paris, 1947), I could not refrain from drawing paral-
lels with the Rule of St Benedict.

in an Ashram, found in a South African Cistercian monastery a way of life which to him appeared truly realistic; a way of unifying a life of prayer while making an effectual contribution to the development of a country and its people. He has stated very clearly that his life-style was formed by his encounter with the Cistercians. Today, estimates of the number of monks vary between one and a half million and four and a half million in India; they are numerous in Cambodia, in Thailand and elsewhere, and are very diversified, especially in India. There are some in the vicinity of almost all the Christian monasteries I have visited, and I have lost no opportunity of contact with them and of learning what is common between their monasticism and our own.[8] Certainly one must not idealize, either theirs or ours. In Indonesia, which is characteristically Muslim, there are still Buddhists who, as in other places, become monks to merit for themselves or for others. And a Cistercian of this region said to me: "Sometimes they make us blush, their poverty, their devotion, their silence, their detachment, their gravity, their freedom from mediocrity."

Whatever be the truth of the matter, Hindu and Buddhist monasticism exerts a real influence at present on the life of the peoples in several of these countries, and sometimes on the Christian monks as well. For example, the book of Hermann Pratikto on *Ramayana,* published at Djakarta in 1962, presents an Indonesian adaptation of the legend of this wise and pious Hindu king. Monasticism plays a large part in this book and it has been read in the refectory of a Christian monastery. A Cistercian told me that his vocation originated from his grandfather's reading this legend to him as a child. This type of religious tradition has left its mark more or less definitely on many imaginative minds even among Christians.

The Council has made it unnecessary for Catholics to justify their approach to Hinduism and Buddhism. It is part of

8. Precise information will be found for example in the article of F. Martin, "Le bonze cambodgien" in *France-Asia, Revue mensuelle,* 114-115 (Nov.-Dec., 1955): 409-415.

that "encounter of religions" and "first steps in dialogue" toward which many are now moving.[9] It takes for granted the admission that a good wealth of truth can be tapped from these religions.[10] For monasticism, with which we are here concerned, there is a similar duty. There are many areas of resemblance between Christian and Hindu monasticism; for instance, their historical evolution, their practices and life-style and above all their spiritual attitude. At the same time there are certainly differences. For example, Buddhist meditation is a concentration of the spirit on itself, whereas Christian monastic tradition holds that meditation is dialogue with God in reading the Bible and in prayer."[11] Some Hindu ascetical practices are certainly beneficial, as is now being recognised with regard to Yoga.

Attempts at closer relations between Christian and Hindu monks go back some way. History's most famous example is that of the Jesuit, Robert de Nobili, who, in the first half of the seventeenth century adopted the costume and partly ere-mitic, partly pilgrim life led by the Durus, the Swamis and the Sanyassis in India. Misunderstood, exiled, and accused, he yet paved a way, but there were none to follow. He was defended by Dom Michel, a Benedictine of Monte Cassino, before the Pontifical Commission examining his case. This "beggar clothed with the sun" in his saffron colored robe had marked out a way.[12] It was to be rediscovered in our own day by the Abbé Monchanin whom Fr de Lubac once described as a "monk with a special mission." "He is one of those

9. Cf. Hendrik Kraemer, *World Cultures and World Religions: The Coming Dialogue* (Philadelphia, 1960); Arend T. van Laeuwen, *Christianity in World Religions: The Meeting of the Faith of East and West* (New York, 1964); E. Cornelis, *Valeurs chrétiennes des religions non chrétiennes* (Paris, 1965). From the Hindu point of view, S. Radhakrishnan, *Eastern Religions and Western Thought* (New York, 1959). On the subject of this dialogue the Secretariat for non-Christians has now published a useful brochure: *Vers la recontre des religions. Suggestions pour le dialogue* (Typographie Polyglote Vaticane, 1967); the English edition is entitled *Towards the Meeting of Religions: Suggestions for Dialogue*. This General section will be followed by a brochure treating of more particular problems.

10. J. Moffitt, *art. cit.*, p. 78.

11. Cf. J. Sudbrack, "Christliche und Buddhistische Meditation" in *Geist und Leben* 40 (1967): 144-154.

12. Cf. V. Cronin, *A pearl to India: The Life of Roberto de Nobili* (London, 1959).

men apart, the first fruits of eternity, who fulfil the indispensible service of pure worship, preaching the one thing necessary even by their silence, and pointing to the parousia as the one thing to be longed for, the one thing absorbing all longing."[13] A Benedictine of Kergonan (France) joined him. They have published a book entitled *Hermits of Saccidananda,* with preface written by Dom Jacques Winandy.[14] Dom Henri Le Saulx has since written several books on the dialogue between Christians and Hindus.[15] This is not the place to assess these writings, but we must grant them the merit of courage. Fr de Lubac said that he himself owes everything to his contact with the Abbé Monchanin. Even today this man of God is well remembered in India by many religious men. He has left more than just a memory; he is a living influence. I have even heard it said that "there was much divinity in him." He has not been without disciples. He had in mind "the contemplative life in India as a remote preparation for Indian contemplative life, which will give rise to mystics and doctors of this new Greece."[16] In the hermitage at Saccidananda he formed Fr Francis Mahieu, a Belgian Cistercian from Scourmont, and Fr Bede Griffiths, an English Benedictine from Prinknash. Together these two men founded the Kurisumala Ashram, in Kerala, and Fr Griffiths has written a fine book about this, called *Christian Ashram.*[17] This monastery has grown and has now made a foundation of its own. The Liturgy is celebrated in the Syro-Malanker rite, which the monks have restored at the request of their bishop. Recently the liturgical Commission of the Episcopal Conference has asked them to begin thinking about "a new Indian rite." This is a tremendous

13. H. de Lubac, *Images de l'Abbé Monchanin* (Paris, 1967), p. 109.

14. Tournai-Paris: Casterman, 1956. [Volume 51 of the CS Series is to be a biography of Jules Monchanin. *In Quest of the Absolute*—ed.]

15. *Sagesse hindoue, mystique chrétienne: Du védanta à la Trinité* (Paris: Centurion, 1965); *La recontre d'hindouisme et du Christianisme* (Paris, 1966); *Une Messe aux sources du Gange* (Paris: Seuil, 1967).

16. H. de Lubac, *Images,* p. 93.

17. *Christian Ashram*: *Essays towards an Hindu-Christian Dialogue* (London, 1966), French tr., *L'Inde et le Christ* (Mulhouse: Salvador, 1967). See *id.,* "Monastic Life in India to-day" in *Monastic Studies* 4 (1966): 117-136; C. Conio, "Monachisme oecuménique en Inde" in *Bulletin du Cercle Saint-Jean-Baptiste* 7 (1967): 121-128; S. Dutt, *Buddhist Monks and Monasteries of India* (London, 1962).

task, and will take years to mature, but it is full of promise
for the future, as Fr Mahieu wrote to me. The monks have
adopted the dress, diet, attitudes of prayer, Yoga exercises,
and, as much as possible, the life style of Hindu monasticism.
The result is that the religious-minded Hindus gladly come to
this monastery, and even take part in its prayer. There is
economic expansion all round, and people come from great
distance to the village hospital conducted by Dr Baker, an
English Quaker, and his wife, a Hindu Melchite. Fr Griffiths,
even while he forms the young monks, keeps up useful contacts with representatives of the religious traditions of Hinduism. Through a chance conversation in England with one such
person, I have learned that the Kurisumala Ashram is very
influential.

This is not an isolated incident. There are others. Still we
should recognize that contacts are, on the whole, rare, and
that prejudice continues on both sides. Sometimes such prej-
udices are serious and it would seem that a better mutual
understanding could reduce or remove them. It is certainly
true that the problem of religious interrelationship is further
complicated in some countries by political problems. And yet
possibilities of contact are open from the moment one is
convinced of their utility. I have always been made very welcome in pagodas and Buddhist monasteries. In one of these,
a kind of mother-house and formation center for the young
or for prospective Bonzes, the superior, an elderly man, received us formally, offered us tea, showed us around himself
and answered our questions regarding meditation, private and
public confession, practices of austerity, reading and many
other matters. I was struck by the number of similarities
existing between this monasticism and our own, beside basic
differences; but I must admit here that the Christian monk
who was my interpreter and who had been living for twenty
years at a distance of only twenty miles was learning all this
for the first time just as I was. In another place, a bonze took
me to the cell where he lived alone, quite near the community
but separate from it, and showed me the hermitage where
others come in turn to spend some time in solitude. In another
Buddhist monastery the superior, to help us learn, let us

hear tape recordings of pagoda chants—really tonal recitations, for these bonzes do not sing. And lastly, another, as a mark of friendship and gesture of farewell, willingly wrote at my request, in the script of his country with a transcription into European characters, the "Prayer of the Bonzes," the triple invocation to Buddha, to the Law and to the community. Another bonze asked me with all simplicity: "Are you happy in your monastic life? I myself am very happy in the pagoda monastery."

Certainly, the first need is to educate Christians—who form in these countries a minority group, and as such do assume a defensive attitude. It is necessary for them to see their monks maintaining friendly relations with Buddhist monks, perhaps even resembling them somewhat, without losing their own identity. It is twenty years since Dom Thomas Ohm strove for real understanding of Buddhism and drew the attention of Christians to the assessment made by Asiatics on the Western character of Christianity.[18] Such an endeavor has remained the exception. It would certainly be according to the mind of Vatican II for this to be taken up again and intensified. In the West a work like this can be done either on a learned[19] or on a popular level.[20] In Asia itself, however, it ought to be carried out by Asiatic Christians and Western Christians in exchanges of information through books and through direct contact. A fine historical example of the integration of Buddhist narratives into Christian monastic literature is furnished in the "Life of St Josaphat and Baarlam," which has been aptly described as "the most famous book in universal literature,"[21] and which is really the life of Buddha Christianized. In the monastic breviary we are still reading passages from it

18. Cf. H. de Lubac, *La rencontre de bouddhisme et de l'Occident* (Paris, 1952), p. 257.

19. A. Ravier, *et al.*, *La mystique et les mystiques* (Paris-Bruges: Desclée de Brouwer, 1964) with preface by H. de Lubac. See the review of this work by F. de Grunne in *Rythmes du monde* 40 (1966), 139-149.

20. An example of this can be found in the missal and book of prayers published by Abbé R. Berthier, under the title *Vivante parole*, containing a collection of extracts from various authors, Catholic, Protestant, Buddhists and unbelievers.

21. H. Gregoire, "L'auteur géorgien du Roman de Barlaam et Joasaph" in *Le Flambeau* 46 (1963): 21 and following, listed in *Cahiers de civilisation médiévale* 9 (1966), 441, no. 2114.

every year on the feast of All the Saints of the Benedictine Order (November, 13).

In Indonesia today there is a Christianized Ramayana. Light would be thrown on some themes by research in this field. Fr de Lubac has written that "Origen breathed the atmosphere of Alexandria and absorbed its ideas, some of them foreign, some coming from the heart of India," but "for him, this gnostic air is purified and transformed into spirituality. Thus filtered, ordered, spiritualized, interiorized, this approach becomes part of the broad current of tradition. To prove our point we will cite here only two great names, those of St Gregory of Nyssa and St Bernard, both of whom were certainly influenced by Origen. St Bernard returns again and again to the different ways in which the Word, himself remaining unchanged, appears to men according to each one's dispositions and degree of preparation. Others too have drawn upon these texts, and it must be admitted that their thought affords a rather curious resemblance with Buddhist theory, suggesting the question of a common source or borrowing."[22]

It has been necessary to speak here at some length of Hinduism and Buddhism, although in very general terms, because it was originally from India that these two religions, which exerted the widest possible influence, spread over the whole of Asia. Zen Buddhism spread to China and from there to Japan. Its monasticism is very lofty.[23] There is no question of seeking a syncretism which would be as unworthy of Christianity, as of the religions of the Far East. But as Fr de Lubac again says after pages nuancing "the discernment, openness and envelopment" which Buddhism demands of Christians, "there are many Christian things that could flourish in Buddhism!"[24] Monasticism must play its part in this work which

22. H. de Lubac, *Aspects du bouddhisme* (Paris, 1951), pp. 122-123.

23. H. M. Enomiya-Lassalle SJ, *Zen, Weg zur Erleuchtung* (Vienna, 1960); H. M. Lassalle SJ, *Le zen, chemin d'illumination* (Desclée de Brower, 1965); P. Wienphal, *The Mother of Zen—A Brief Account of Zazen* (New York, 1964); other works have been analyzed by T. Merton in *Collectanea Cisterciensia* 29 (1967): 181-190.

24. *La rencontre . . .*, p. 253. A recent example of a meeting between Buddhism and the thought of a Christian philosopher, Gabriel Marcel, is found in Sally Donnelly, *Marcel and Buddha,* for which T. Merton has written a very thought-provoking preface.

is at once a work of understanding and charity. I could not
help thinking of this on the occasion of an unforgettable visit
I made with a few Indonesian Cistercians to the Temple of
Barabudur: a huge, harmoniously proportioned place of more
than ten stone terraces engraved with bas-reliefs representing
the whole Buddhist mythology, with niches sheltering the
statue of Buddha at meditation, also of "stupas" within which
was again the seated Buddha. The nearer you go to the top
of this immense stone pyramid the less decoration, sculpture
and statuary you find. Everything becomes simpler, purer.
At the very top there is room only for the great awning on
a terrace from which one looks out over a wide panaroma,
and closer at hand over hundreds of people lost in meditation.
When a young Christian monk of this country took his place
thus alongside a Buddha, and in the same posture, it was a
symbol of the encounter of two contemplative traditions.

OTHER RELIGIOUS TRADITIONS AND HISTORICAL FACTS

Indian traditions are not the only ones which have influenced
the religious and psychological characteristics of countries in
which Christian monasticism is now being implanted. All these
countries over a span of hundreds and thousands of years have
had relations with China, and have been more or less subject
to her influence. At present there are Chinese everywhere—
Confusionists, Taoists, Christians or Communists. The depth
of the traces left by this past on the mental, social, and familial
structures of a whole generation were brought home to me on
the occasion of my meeting with an old professor of Chinese at
a university. The son of a Mandarin and a convert from Con-
fucianism to Christianity, he remained an ardent admirer of
Confucius and his teaching, and at the same time he was pas-
sionately hostile to Taoism and Buddhism. He explained to me
at length the twelve Chinese characters which sum up the Confucian doctrine, showing them to me in a book which he had
written in the course of his study. He even had the goodness to
offer me two scrolls on which, as they are enrolled, these twelve
letters are to be seen painted upon silk in designs full of meaning. He could see in the doctrine of "heaven" and its implica-
tions stepping stones for the doctrine of the Incarnation and

many possible points of agreement with Christianity. He directs a kindergarten, whose main building and garden were arranged in Chinese style. In the true Confucian spirit he holds to the veneration of his father and ancestors. Alas, their portraits surrounded by Chinese works of art in exquisite taste were placed beside the altar on which all the Christian ornaments, imported from the West, were completely mediocre. But I admired never-theless this touching alliance of Confucian souvenirs and Christian piety.

Another religion more or less widely represented in the region is Islam. The village closest to one of the monasteries which I recently visited in India was entirely Moslem. In Indonesia the greatest part of the population is Moslem. And one at least of the officially recognized languages of the country is so deeply influenced by Arabic that it was easy to detect many words from the Hebrew Bible when we cele-brated the Divine Office. And yet elements from primitive religions or from Buddhism intermingle with that derived au-thentically from the Koran. In the Philippines there is the opposite situation, for the majority of the population is Cath-olic while Islam is present and very active. Imported a cen-tury and a half before the Spaniards arrived, it left its roots, and the President of the Republic expressed public recognition of its benefits at the inauguration of the first mosque in the Philippines, in June, 1967.[25]

It goes without saying that monasticism will have to take into account all these component elements in the religious make-up of each country, and it is also important to state all these facts before formulating the problems which present themselves. It could be said there are two aspects to be con-sidered. On the one hand there are in Asia strongly devel-oped religious traditions, doctrinally elaborated from a period of antiquity going back well beyond Christianity. They have been given extensive expression of real quality in art and literature. Several of them have a monasticism of their own, and while there is no question of imitating this, we realize that Christian monasticism can be enriched by some of its

25. Summary of the discourse in *Philippine News Digest* (June 12, 1967).

religious insights, some of its forms of thought or observance. On the other hand these different traditions are sometimes to a greater or lesser extent mixed, mutually influenced and even vitiated. As well as openness and sympathy, then, one needs discernment.

Finally, everywhere the most recent of what we could call the "geological or archeological foundations" of Asiatic religion have come from Christians. Certainly in India evangelization began from the very earliest times, and Nestorian churches were to be found shortly afterwards in China. But it was only in the colonial period that Christianity was implanted and spread to some extent. The Latin church came first with missionaries of St Francis Xavier's period; then came the Anglican church with the arrival of Englishmen. In the Philippines Christianity took the form of the Spanish Catholicism of the sixteenth century and the North American Christian religions of the twentieth; in Cambodia, Vietnam and Laos, nineteenth-century French Catholicism shaped the Christian mission. Indonesian Christianity of Calvinist Holland has been supplemented by a staunch, if timid Catholicism, which is today assertive, but sound.[26]

Monasticism was everywhere stamped by the particular characteristic of the Catholicism in the colonizing nation. Almost inevitably there has been some degree of compromise with the colonial powers and this has recently provoked negative reaction. But it remains true that the Church and the monastic life in Asia today have a strong European stamp. Moreover, this influence is strengthened by the Congregation for the Propagation of the Faith and the College of Propaganda. Roman Canon Law has received the same esteem as theology.

The Western character of the Church in Asia is then a fact. In spite of an ancient tradition in part of India and in several other countries, the influence of the Christian East was not, and is not, as strong as that of the Latin world. In particular, there has been a lag in the liturgical and contemplative

---

26. At the opening of the twentieth century, Christianity entered as an element in this religious syncretism which is "caodaism."

sensitivity to the Orient. Missionaries of the nineteenth century along with their fervor and devotion brought the theological ideas proper to their time and their respective countries. Moreover, they showed a fine spirit of charity in the fields of health, education and general development; so that as a result, while people praise Hindu morality and Moslem religious spirit, they single out the economic effectiveness of Christianity. The Church is active and monasticism's traditional role of worship—which is evident in the Asiatic religions—hardly appears at all.

This past as we have described it is still influencing the psychological attitude of many Catholics. Those who come from the West often display an evident superiority complex in their attitude. "They have come to serve us as our masters," a monk once said to me. A Jesuit in Japan recently expressed some ideas which apply equally well elsewhere: "Why are missionaries always sympathetic with the liberal democratic party in Japan? Why do they take as an attack on themselves anything said directly against capitalism and capitalist countries? Why do they show no appreciation for the efforts made by socialist countries to improve the conditions of the workers and the poor. . . . The main obstacle to a just appreciation of Christianity by the Japanese is the image it gives of itself; over-confident in its self-sufficiency, over-Western, over-capitalist."[27] Then again the inferiority complex of the autochtonous peoples towards Westerns is often accompanied by real trust and wareness of need. The missionary spirit has not always developed strongly. Their Christianity remains a minority, estranged from the life of the rest of the country and undeveloped. Where monasticism exists, and in the measure that it exists, it shares in all these characteristics.

Finally, any treatment of monasticism, as of other manifestations of Catholicism, should consider the contemporary development with its many complexities. Firstly, there is the influence of Western technical progress. In Japan it has made great headway and everywhere else it is showing some pro-

27. J. Ribas SJ, "The Church seen through Japanese Eyes" in *The Japan Missionary Bulletin* (Jan. 1967), quoted in *Herder Correspondence* (English edition, April, 1967), p. 131.

gress. This alone is cause for rejoicing, but in our opinion increased wealth and industrialization are not the answer to every need. A Hindu whom I met at one of Europe's large airports, pointed to the milling, well-fed but anxious looking, crowd and said "India has her exterior poverty but here the destitution lies within man himself. . . ."

At the same time there is the creation of "national" cultures in countries of various racial origins and different civilizations. For instance, in the Indonesian archipelago Java has its own culture and so has Sumatra, Bali and the other islands; but it is not an Indonesian culture or language in the sense that it is not the same everywhere. The creation of new cultures by the governments that have taken over from colonial powers, involves two aspects. On the one hand a national language is gradually being enforced. There is some resistance here but the measure seems inevitable. On the other hand traditional values are still respected, and even sometimes rediscovered. People are showing new awareness of them and renewed assurance in them. Works of art are being restored and protected, art galleries enriched, and there is a general fostering of handicraft. Folk dances and other expressions of traditional culture are encouraged, and though the artificial and the superficial appear at first, the trend itself cannot fail to produce results in time. There is a dimension of infinite charm in the combination of modern technique with a typically Asiatic aesthetic. An example of this is provided by the countless "jeepneys" in the vast city of Manila: these jeeps, laden with ornaments and garlands, and decorated with multicolored paintings—like the buses—are so many motorized "calesas" and look as poetic as the old one-horse buggies that we find as we get out into the country.

All the diverse forces, so contradictory in appearance, constitute problems for monasticism as for the Church. Until now the Church has been a Latin Chruch. The current creation of liturgical languages with melodies adapted to each country, poses many questions. I understand that bishops and Episcopal Conferences have asked the monasteries to assist in solving them. The project of a Vietnamese Mass which the Benedictines of Tien-An were working on a few years ago had the merit of showing what could be done in this field.[28] Here we are broaching the complicated area of adaptation and many sound ideas have already been voiced.[29] Some certainly prefer to speak of this trend as creativity. The Church will have to find ways of growing into the natural and traditional riches of every culture, and monasticism will have its part to play in this endeavour. Its present effort here must be intensified.

Finally, there must be no misunderstanding of the role of modern ideologies, especially Communism. Whatever be the immediate political situation in each country, the Communist influence is present and active everywhere in Asia.

This cannot fail to have results, but we shall not attempt to predict them here. Our point is that the result must certainly be taken into account. Some traditional values, some social, psychological, familial, and political structures will be transformed or eliminated, and separation from the West will be accentuated. In the cultural sphere the chief victim, or at any rate the first, from now on, is likely to be "the old Confucianist world" as it has been called. We recall here Pope Paul's message to China in January of 1967 which referred to "the change-over from the old static traditional forms of culture to its new and inevitable forms deriving from modern industrial and social structures."[30] On the other hand the appearance of neo-Buddhist sects, like the Soka Gakkai in a country like Japan, convinces us that in spite of, or perhaps because of technical progress a profound religious void is now being experienced, especially by the poor and middle class. The Church will have to make good this loss.[31] Some think that the West on the whole will gradually "be trans-

28. The text has been published in *La Feuille des oblates,* (Abbey of Sainte-Marie at Paris and Saint-Maurice et St-Maur at Clervaux, 1965), pp. 45-57.

29. See, for example, Parnananda Divarkar SJ, "Once again, the Intellectual Apostolate" in *The Clergy Monthly Supplement* (June-July, 1964), pp. 61-66; M. Dhavamony SJ, "Christian Experience and Hindu Spirituality" in *Gregorianum* 48(1967): 776-791, has analysed with great precision the successive factors which have determined the different philosophical and religious aspects of Hinduism.

30. Text in *Documentation catholique* 44 (1967), no. 219.

31. From the *Bulletin du Centre de Réflexion sur le Monde non occidental* (CRM) 7 (May, 1967): 9.

formed through its encounter with other cultures and civilizations, other modes of thinking, other religions, and that this transformation will be affected in proportion to the depth of the discovery. It is quite clear that the nations to whom the West rather condescendingly offers its logic and techniques have quite another conception of them, and to be objective we must ask ourselves whether this latter attitude does not reflect a truer and perhaps a superior point of view than that which has so long prevailed in the West. For example, the Oriental approach to science is profoundly different; it gives rise to a pure and strong animism which some nations, like modern Japan, now excelling in technical and scientific development, do not seem to grasp. Hence, perhaps, a new possibility of realizing harmony between science and humanism."[32]

These, then, are the perspectives of the future. At the present time, the solution of problems already obvious seems to demand neither return to the pure Asiatic past, nor imitation of the West, but rather the creation of Asiatic cultures which conform at once to the psychology and traditions of the different peoples and to new trends, thanks in part to the use they make of modern technology and its consequences in the field of thought and action. A magnificent opportunity is being offered to Asia; in this, monasticism has its modest place. It must remain open to this important work.

PSYCHOLOGICAL FACTORS

The fact that first calls for attention is that vocations to the monastic life, among both men and women, do exist. Their authenticity is occasionally guaranteed by the opposition with which they meet; but in contrast with what happens on other continents, this opposition does not come from the family, at least when the family is Christian. But when young people leave a seminary or a novitiate of an active order to enter a monastery, they arouse legitimate and well-meant opposition

---

32. M. Meylon, "Les problèmes d'organisation et de structure de l'entreprise industrielle" in *Document d'information et de gestion* 2 (November, 1966), 5.

from rectors, spiritual directors and missionaries. I was told that one of these young people had come "to converse with the all powerful God," another to live "in joyous silence," yet another summed up his program in three words "I want to sing, to pray, to work." He did not feel urged to teach, to preach, to build, or to go about. When I asked, as is asked in other parts of the world: "Why have you come to the monastery?", I have met frequent insistence on a desire for leisure and for joy.

Why is it that Christians feel this attraction towards contemplative life when they learn it is being lived in their country? Can one say that Asiatics are "naturally" contemplative? One ought to be extremely cautious of making such a statement. The truth expressed herein applies to the whole Church. We should note here in passing that it is normal for a proportion of those entering monasteries as adults not to remain permanently. Some of those who face the exigencies of monastic life will become aware that it is not for them. This is good. The life will have left some impression on them. It is good too that here and there we find authentic calls to the eremitic life. Asia's problem lies in the fascination of the priesthood for many. Families regard it as bestowing prestige, in fact almost status. The nineteenth-century missionaries true to the theology and piety of the day encouraged this trend. When you hear that a young monk will or will not be directed to study for the priesthood for which intelligence or sound judgment fit him, you wonder whether these qualities so necessary for the pastoral ministry, should be considered less so for the difficult adventure of facing God in the contemplative life. The determining factor should be, not the degree of education so much as its type. Is it too simple a solution, then, simply to send monks to a neighboring seminary to be educated? Even if excellent courses are provided by the curriculum, that does not form monks. On the other hand the desire to study which is very strong in some, may show that the religious is more or less consciously seeking promotion. The existence of vocations should not make us forget that they often raise problems.

The first factor distinguishing monastic life from other forms of life in the Church is traditionally *separation from the world.* This immediately poses the question of relations with the world. Now Asia finds less difficulty in reconciling separation from the world and union with it than some of our Western ideas and practices would give us to think. The differences between nature on one hand and the village, or even the town, on the other, is less sharp than with us.

Easterners have a wonderful capacity for embracing the whole order of reality without setting up precise distinctions and boundaries. Concerning the distinction between solitude and openness to the world, I have heard it said that "this is a problem only in the West; you can be alone with God wherever you are." In Rome's recent legislation the emphasis on enclosure with its walls and grilles, seems exaggerated; observances which are meant to be supple have been made rigid. They have been marked by flexibility even in the West for the greater part of our history. Our Asian brothers may help us to envisage what one might call "open enclosure," with reduction of the many detailed prescriptions which aim at foreseeing and settling everything. These minutiae can easily enslave us.

We are dealing here with a mental attitude very deep in the Asian spirit. It is difficult to pin-point, but has importance and practical consequences, especially in the area of family relationships. The Asiatic solidarity with family and society is keenly felt. The family, moreover, is very extensive, comprising in itself quite a vast society. Someone explained to me that this solidarity embraces parents and relatives on both sides of the family to the fourth degree, over three or four generations. Grandparents alone know the lineage completely, and instruct their descendants in it. In such a context, family relationships, and the visits to be made and received will be very different from those of the West. On the other hand such a developed sense of family makes people very alert to any discrimination within the community. When over-accentuated, the distinction between priests and non-priests is just as offensive as that which existed between monks and brothers until recently. The unification of communities is no less necessary in Asia than elsewhere. The introduction of classes deriving from the Middle Ages in the West is purely artificial in the far East.

Marriage is often regarded as an alliance between two fam-

ilies, and there is a strong element of this in the natural priority
given to the bond of love. This brings out the full meaning of
what St Benedict has said about the monk not favoring or
unduly defending a blood relation, but this family solidarity
contributes to our understanding of a universal fraternity.
Community life is relished by all, reflecting as it does man's
whole nature. *Voluntary celibacy* is to be weighed and justified
against this background as a form of marriage, important and
natural, but different. On this point our Asian brethren help
us to rediscover a communitarian concept of "celibacy for
the kingdom," which is at once evangelical and traditional.
Recent theology stresses this, just as Vatican II recalled it.
The importance attributed to large families helps toward our
appreciation of the immense value of spiritual fecundity, but
this sense of racial solidarity may also be an impediment to
unity. It is allegedly difficult for different races and nations to
live together, and to elect from among themselves a superior
whom all will accept with good grace. But this difficulty is
general; the European countries have not solved it. Finally,
hospitality with all its exigencies is part of the Asiatic make-
up: to welcome visitors, to converse with them, work with
them, and spend one's time with them. The bond between
charity and asceticism is more spontaneous in Asia than with
us.

In this overall life-style, the *role of the word* is very great.
While the inner rhythm of peace provides a possibility for the
life of prayer, the need for communication leads to fraternity.
Balance demands effort. Due to the position of the cell I occupied in one monastery's guest house I could not help over-
hearing during the course of the days the conversation of men
working in the adjacent timber yard. These men came from a
village where nothing remarkable ever happened, but they
always had plenty to talk about. I could not understand the
conversation, but it must have been very pleasant. They had
many a laugh, and I often heard them singing. But it does not
follow from this that Asiatics have no great capacity for recollection. I have been told that the Abbot General of the Cistercians was impressed by the silence of the bonzes, and is still
referring to it. This is just another example of the way in

which we have hardened and reduced to rigid regulations things that ought to be aspirations of the heart. We have our designations of "strict silence" and "perpetual silence." Even when Asiatics speak, their conversation is very different from ours. They make a good use of proverbs, they are fond of long discussion, sometimes about nothing in particular, but arising from the simple joy of being together. Thus can silence be a fruit of recollection, and speech a medium of charity.

Another trait in the psychology of Asiatics derives from their sense of time and work. In this they differ appreciatively from us. One day out in the country when our train was stopping all the time, my monk companion remarked that if this had happened in Europe the passengers would have got up from their seats without delay and gone to make enquiries, but here no one even seemed to notice. Time seemed free and open. I wondered what was the horarium at the monastery we were going to. I noticed several clocks when we got there, and they were all going except the one in the kitchen of the guest house. This was one which only the Asiatics used and evidently they were under no pressure of need to know the time. After Fr de Lubac's short visit to India he recounted his meeting with Abbé Monchanin, adding this comment: "I found him very poor (one simple detail: he did not even have a watch)."[33] Now, can we regard this as just a detail or proof of poverty? The heart too has become more free in its attitude toward that element of the world which is measured time. It has been known for Asian monks caught in the exigencies of a Western horarium to say: "We have no longer any time to live." And one of them characterized his fellow countrymen as "happy, all right, but a bit lazy." "More brainy than brave;" another admitted to me, adding, "We work slowly, but we do work." There is a splendid Javenese proverb: "Even an overworked angel can no longer smile." Experience persuades me to temper the severity of these charming judgments. I have seen Asiatics working hard, and I am not only referring to monks; but they are not enslaved to minute time-tables in the way we are, and so they are more respectful of that which can be lost

33. *Images de l'abbé Monchanin,* p. 88.

under the domination of time. This is not solely an empirical factor in daily life. It is a conclusion which has been recently noted in relation to the great economic evolutions, in connection with the "acceleration of history" and the "race against time." "There is plenty of talk about the conquest of space, but not much about the conquest of time. Now, writing, printing, books, radio, television, the network of information by telecommunication stations or satellites are stages marking this conquest of time by humanity, and yet for a large area of the world, this notion of the speeding up of evolution, or the conquest of time, has no reality or significance at all. There is no even balance, then, between the different types of the human race. . . ."[34] On the ordinary level of monastic life let us be careful not to force our Asiatic brethren to adopt our pace; there is no struggle against time in this going to God of which St Benedict speaks. Let us avoid overtaxing them, or imposing on them our interior or exterior rhythms. And if they are content with little, we should let them be poor and happy in the way God wants them to be. What about the proverb that says: "There is rice every day."

We have already found it necessary to allude to the problem of poverty. This certainly goes beyond the frontiers of monasticism; it is a problem for the whole church, and is beginning to be felt everywhere in religious life, especially by the young. This very point is one of the most reassuring signs of the vitality of Catholicism in the post-Vatican II age. But here and now we are only examining it in relation to monks and nuns. While we are aware of the urgency of the Christian contribution to economic and social developments in all fields, we cannot fail to be alert to the call of the Council to this "collective witness of poverty" which religious should give. I have heard the question put this way: "If monks do the same things as others in the domain of spiritual and material activities, what is the good of being a monk?" This helps

34. J. de Rosnay in *Compte rendu des assemblées générales du 8 décembre 1966, de Centre d'Étude des Conséquences générales des grandes Techniques nouvelles* (CTN) *et du CRM*, p. 27.

us to understand the aspiration for a simple monastic life which is coming to light in many places. Sometimes this is a problem proper to Westerners, and artificially introduced into Asia after the Council—but shall we say that this is always the case? Some Westerners are too easily inclined to think that wealth in a monastery is scandalous, whereas Asiatics would have so deep an understanding of God and his mystery that they would realize that money spent on buildings is spent for him. Certainly, this reason may have been true in the Middle Ages in the West, but there has been an irreversible evolution throughout the whole world. Communism alone would produce problems for Asia of which ancient history knew nothing. And is not the question being asked now more than ever before: What do the poor think about religion? Is it still necessary to insist, in Asia as much as everywhere else, on interior poverty, because of a tendency to give too much importance to the facade—of individuals, as much as of buildings—to their reputation, to the impression they are making, to their desire to be always "saving face." And this is not without repercussions on the psychology of humility, self-accusation and correction. On all these points, the Benedictine rule would have been written rather differently in these countries. The historical forms in which the mystery of humility is expressed are not to be imposed everywhere.

Finally, there is a psychological characteristic in many Asiatics which is difficult to define, and which constitutes a marked difference between them and many Westerners. Let me try to convey some idea of this, for it is not less favorable to monasticism than several of the points already mentioned. On one side, in ideas and doctrines, there is less precision, perhaps, than in the religious thought of the West, especially among Catholics. This has been mentioned, for example, with regard to Hinduism,[35] and someone has said of Buddhism that it has a highly developed mysticism, but no theology.[36] Whatever be the case with other religions, this is certainly the attitude found among Christians—both in theory and in practice. While

35. J. Moffitt, *art. cit.*, pp. 76-78.
36. A. Bareau, quoted by H. de Lubac, *La rencontre . . .*, p. 279.

this is not free from disadvantage it has nevertheless its own value. I have heard it said with regard to Westerners: "They have defined God, they know exactly who he is". This Asiatic sensitivity to mystery is truly worthwhile, and we should do well to imitate it. Among them one does not find, as with many of us, an obsession with the practical.

On the other hand, they clearly have a very fine *poetic sense*—matching the practical, and yet surpassing it and giving it significance. Now, poetry and imagination are authentic means of access to that Truth whose depth and beauty can never be gauged by reason and speculative understanding alone. This poetic gift explains the part played by mythological narratives in religion, art, literature and life as a whole, not forgetting the cinema. It seems that after the United States, it is India which produces the most films, and these give to mythology a place which we of the West find disconcerting. In Asia everyone enjoys telling stories, whether of their own or of another's composition. A monk confided to me that at the parlor when trying to comfort someone in trouble he sometimes tells him a story. "For the moment the poor man forgets his trouble in admiration for the great hero whose deeds he has been hearing. He smiles, and this is all that is needed. He does not protest that the story is not real." Among them one would not often hear what one western monk said of another: "What a pity he's a poet!"

In the East monks are very easily satisfied, and always joyous. They are intelligent and able to handle problems—but they can easily manage without them. Why should we impose ours then, or induce Easterners to create some of their own? In one of the languages there is a word of Islamic origin which can take on Christian meaning in the monastic life; it is the word for giving oneself in complete trust to the Providence of God. Who is going to say that there is a trace of fatalism here? The word can also mean "Thy will be done."

In short without prejudice to trends such as technical progress, which are of European or American origin and now universal, the Asian has deep rooted propensities for the monastic life, under the surface veneer left from

the colonial era. These are both psychological and spiritual, and derive in part from the non-Christian religious
traditions and in part independently of them and from
the sole fact of a mentality willed for them by God. It would
be a pity if the Church did not respond to this natural disposition.

THE MONASTIC CONTRIBUTION

What is the stage of monastic development in Asia? To ask
this question is not to criticize what has been accomplished
by the policy of a period which has only just passed, and in
which we all certainly shared; but we now have to ask ourselves
if we are going to continue along the same road.

Have we first asked ourselves what form of monasticism
these Christians need. Before actually going to Asia, and after
arriving there, did we make a point of studying its history,
religions and languages? We seem rather to have imposed on
them the only form of monasticism that we knew. We brought
along whatever was specific to different countries and institutions in the West—though all of this was determined by national
histories and psychologies that were foreign to the East. When
we had been there for some time did we ask ourselves whether
we needed to change anything we had brought or imported?
Did we ask *what* changes were needed—and how far they
should go? Did we really listen? Did we observe? Did we learn
by experience? Westerners easily give Asiatics the impression
of not knowing how to listen: "They know everything before-
hand" someone said to me with a smile, "and do not need to
be shown anything." Fr Ribas (quoted above) testifies that
Westerners are over-confident. They really need to learn how
to learn. In the meantime they have succeeded in persuading
the people of these countries that they must imitate whatever
is done in Europe—and monasteries want everything done as
it is in the motherhouse. Once a beginning has been made in a
definite direction it is very difficult to turn back. However,
many and especially the young are now becoming aware of
values that are specifically Asiatic. These are both traditional

and current, as we have shown above. We have no right to
discount them.

A recent historical study of the Cistercian formation in
Ireland during the thirteenth century provides a historical
precedent in this matter we have just been discussing. It was
the period of Stephen of Lexington, Visitor and Reformer of
his Order.[37] A hundred years earlier in that country, ever
tenacious of its own traditions, there had been introduced
methods of formation which had proved their worth on the
continent and in England, and what happened? After a few
generations one finds forms of monasticism totally different
from what was intended.[38] Moreover, the practices of spirituality which had succeeded elsewhere proved quite useless
in Ireland. "By insisting on a form of study rooted in another
culture" (someone has written of Stephen of Lexington) "he
cramped those whom he had tried to help, and not only
lessened their love of study, but probably their charity also."[39]
The same type of thing has happened in our time. One
finds that the details of observance and horarium followed in
the motherhouse are often imposed. What is worse, sometimes
even the mentality of the European members is enforced; for
example their concept of silence. Sometimes we introduced recent concepts of monasticism where older traditions would have
allowed for greater flexibility. There was considerable anxiety
about recruits. Wherever large scale education monopolized
most of the monks' activity, numbers were needed, and obtained. The large scale involvement in education was prejudicial
to the specifically monastic forms of apostolate which are par-

---

37. D. O. O'Dwyer, "The Problem of Education in the Cistercian Order" in
Journal of Religious History 3 (1964-1965): 238-245.

38. Thus we see the Irish Cistercians of the thirteenth century beginning again
to live in wretched wooden huts, conformably to the age-old practice of the
Celtic monks, and not in large buildings in imitation of those on the continent;
"living beyond the cloister in huts wretchedly built solely of branches. . . ."
B. Griesser. "Registrum epistolarum Stephani de Lexington" in *Analecta S. Ordinis
Cisterciensis* 2 (1946): 14; further on, p. 37: "A few are living in common, but
in groups of three or four in little cells gathered together beyond the cloister.
The words *casula* and *casella* recall those 'cells' surviving in so many names of
places in Ireland, under forms such as 'Keil' (Kil)."

39. H. C.'s report of O'Dwyer in *Citeaux* 18 (1967): 168.

ticularly necessary where they do not exist at all. To procure what was needed for the upkeep of their schools, the monks engaged in ventures that absorbed time and energy which they could have used to greater profit.

But wherever contact with the West was broken prematurely, for political or psychological reasons, the evolution which could have been accomplished did not in fact eventuate. As a consequence it is taking longer. The present temptation of Asian monasticism might well be to a kind of neo-colonialism: an imitation of the countries from which monastic life came. There was no general attempt to imitate where what had previously been done in economy, art, piety or theology was better. But there was an effort to revive in Asia the neo-medieval or more accurately pseudo-medieval monasticism of the nineteenth and earlier twentieth century, fostering the myth of great abbeys with their vast buildings and large communities (in fact exceptional). Romanesque and Gothic crypts were even built. It would be a pity, however, if Asia were to become the museum of a West that has vanished—or a conservatory of a pre-conciliar Catholic life. For in fact Vatican II has happened. It has given a definite drive to the creation of new liturgical forms and to a renewed theology and spirituality replenished at the sources. The Council has asked that "the collective witness of poverty" which religious must give should be shown in new forms, and these are to be devised. Moreover, while an economy of abundance and affluence prevails in a large part of the world, poverty remained, and even increased in other regions, sometimes in the wake of war. How far have we responded to this new situation? How far are we ready to get involved?

PERSPECTIVES

Now what course is the future to take? In every country, monasticism is part of the sum total of the reality of the Church. The study of this reality is the province of all with authority and competence. These two do not necessarily go together, they must complement each other. No one person from the outside, or from his own personal point of view, can trace out present and future trends. So all we can do here in regard to monasticism is to indicate the attitude that is to be avoided and stimulate confidence and courage.

The worst line of action would be to declare: "We Asiatics differ from other peoples in this matter. We are quite capable of imitating the West, consequently we have no problems." As if the West had none! If this policy was adopted in the recent past, no one has the right to continue it. We must abandon the existing trend if we are to rectify and redirect it. Moreover, wherever possible, there must be new creations. This holds true in two areas: that of spirituality and that of institution.

First of all, it is important to believe in the monastic life and in its specific character, but it is necessary to have a notion of its spirituality that is both traditional and realistic. For example, to imagine that the contemplative life (an expression retained by the Council) requires extraordinary graces would be to draw on an interpretation of "mystical" that is not accepted today. In this regard, the Council and the popes refer to a special vocation, but one whose fulfillment is assured by ordinary grace and ordinary gifts. It is true that an idealistic view of monasticism is sometimes presented. We must retain or rediscover a conception of prayer and asceticism which will suit modern men everywhere. Ideals are not enough here. There has often been a structuring, even an excessive hardening, of spiritual liberty. This liberty must certainly be guided and educated, but not stifled by laws, observances, customs, preoccupation with centralization and uniformity modelled almost always on the norms of the nineteenth-century West.

In the second place it is important to trust in the values proper to Asia, if there is to be an authentic transcultural-ization of contemplative life in the Church. This takes for granted a knowledge of these values and the result will be assured only if those who possess the values are given leave to speak. We must listen to Asiatics, those within the monastery for sure, but also those outside, to have discussions with them without claiming the right of imposing our opinions, to be initiated into their culture, their history, the religious traditions of their countries, to see Angkor or Barabudur not like curious tourists looking for exotic art, but in a humble, interested, sympathetic spirit, eager to know and above all to understand. When I visited one of the museums, there was a young native painter displaying his tiles alongside rooms that were filled with exhibits of ancient Buddhist art. His ultra-modern style and technique did not belie his fully traditional inspiration: mythological themes, religious ceremonies, funerals or cremations, masks, dances, sacred animals, The artist himself told me his whole inspiration came to him from his religion and his silent meditation in the temple. And I admired the fact that an inspiration as traditional as this found expression in so new a medium. He told me also that some of his fellow artists, both Moslem and Christian, were working each in his own sphere along similar lines.

To tell the truth, in private houses or churches I have seen only the worst kind of pre-Huysmans Sulpican art. On this point, too, the Asian Catholic is lagging behind the rest. Sometimes, one has the impression that in these highly civilized and architecturally refined countries where decoration in form and color attains such richness in simplicity, Christians have a monopoly on ugliness. However, in justice we should recognize that monasteries—without exception—give proof of better taste and an authentic search for beauty. It is true that some artists of Asia have modelled their statues of the Mother of God on an Italian madonna. But, when one has prayed before it, one cannot forget the statue of Our Lady of Cambodia at the monastery of Kep. Mary is raising one hand in a gesture which for them is an attitude of prayer. She holds the Child on her hip, as is done in the near and far East—and as the Blessed Virgin would certainly have done. Both Virgin and Child are not typical westerners of today. Artistic research is tending here toward an effort after truth.

It could be one of the functions of monasteries to promote beauty. Another role could be the helping of Asiatic Christians to find a style of prayer in harmony with their interior rhythm, with a place for silent meditation in the celebration of the Divine Office itself, with the time-table, the liturgical language, melodies, gestures and postures proper to each traditional culture.

The type of formation must be adapted to the exigencies of monasticism in its present state in each country. The need to study must be purified, it must be or become a search for God, not a way of fulfilling one's aspiration, even ambition, of worldly promotion or to overcome an inferiority complex. Whenever material work tends to absorb too much time or energy, the horarium will need to be restored to balance to insure time for reflection, reading and silent prayer. And if the objection is made to this or any other modification of observance that "it is less Cistercian," or "less Benedictine," the reply to be made is: "so much the better, if it is more monastic". In simple truth this will be in closer conformity with the Rule of St Benedict. Once we have intelligent formation, monastic in character rather than clerical, based on Holy Scripture, upon a theology which develops a living knowledge of the mysteries of salvation—rather than that learning which reduces these to thesis-form—once we have constant reference to Christ, once we have a sound historical interpretation of the Rule of St Benedict—which should not be too lightly dismissed as a document anachronistic on every point —then indeed we may hope to prepare and foster a vigorous monasticism which will bring strength to the Church in every country.

Asiatic monks will then find equilibrium between what the West has given them and what they are in themselves—and in such a balance there will develop such institutions and observances as are flexible enough to allow the development of the gifts of nature and grace proper to each of the local churches. We must admit that an authentic monastic life can be lived today in forms very different from those to which we are accustomed. Modern monasticism, whether Eastern, Coptic, Greek or Ethopian, gives proof of this. By showing the extent to which things have changed in the past, the knowledge of history would supply enough imagination to predict the shape of the future. The recognition of the values proper to the various types of monasticism, whether Christian or otherwise in the Near and Far East, would also help toward this creative approach. There is nothing against the opinion that contact and exchange with Orthodox monasteries is even more desirable in Asia than elsewhere. They would help us to develop the particular structures and at a deeper level the inner freedom native to Asiatics, and so to supply an adequate corrective to Western influence.

This is a point which must not be passed over in silence. There are several countries experiencing the progressive disappearance of Europeans who have brought and practically imposed their language along with the colonial regime. Here the disappearance of the European languages is not only predictable, but already verified. The majority are obliged to learn the new official language for the whole country as well as their own dialect, so there will be little chance of their studying in addition a European language, whether ancient or modern. There will follow what may be considered from one point of view a cultural decline. Will it be avoided by enrolling children to teach them Latin, Greek, and English, or French? We seem to be getting back, or even to have reached already, the cultural level of the High Middle Ages, when all the books available for reading led back to the Bible, and very few other works. At present there is no complete translation of the Bible in some places. One would like to imagine that this situation will give rise to the translation of recognized books—and not just small devotional books that bring no particular profit—and to the creation of original works. Paul VI has said that one of the roles of the Benedictines is to give the church "books of spirituality" filled with references to and experience of basic religious realities and well adapted to the vigorous fostering of piety.[40] Such a Pope would expect some contribution of a doctrinal char-

---

40. A discourse delivered to Benedictine abbots, October 1, 1966; text in *Acta Apostolicae Sedis* 58 (1966): 888; a poor translation in *Documentation catholique* 63 (1966), col. 1750.

acter to the solution of problems raised by the real or anticipated spread of atheism. A work of this kind presupposes,
of course, that other forms of activity—educational or material do not absorb the monk's time and energy.

After all that has just been said above of the respect due
local cultures, we may be permitted to express the wish that the
young be given the time and the means to familiarize themselves with one of the widely used modern European languages, and to progress therein. In this way through reading
they will have access to the Catholic tradition as expressed
in a literature that is already rich, while awaiting the time
when their country will have a literature of its own. To sacrifice to work the time needed for reading, results only in an
impoverishment of the contemplative spirit. Overworking the
body results quickly in a draining of the mind. On the other
hand the faith and self-awareness of young Asiatics today
will gain nothing by being troubled prematurely, or at any
rate unpreparedly by the interesting but difficult problems
discussed in European and American theological circles. Enlightened faith, intelligent, but not over-intellectual formation,
sound initiation in Scripture and Tradition, a broad and even
universal approach to the role of monasticism in the Church,
would foster spiritual maturity and personal thought, according to individual capacity.

Asia's problems then will affect her institutions as much as
her resources will. Structures already existing probably need
more flexibility, and certainly need more freedom from the
influence of the West. Not that everything must be thrown
out, but only what accords with God's special gifts to Asia's
men and women should be retained. Moreover, in the West
itself any forced legalism, customs covering every detail, over-
centralization and uniformity would only serve to show a
weakened organism striving to protect and prolong what remained of life. In Asia as elsewhere, in fact more than elsewhere, the need is to recover the spiritual liberty which is
traditional to monasticism. This is the task facing the rising
generation of Asiatics, and the responsibility of Westerners
is to give them confidence in themselves and to trust them.

There remains the problem of creating new institutions; new foundations marked by simplification of observances, of economy, of life-style and of cultural form, so that monastic life will be accessible to the peoples of each country who may have neither the wish nor the capacity for the type of formation at present required for those devoted to the contemplative search for God. Communities ought to be rather limited in number and very fraternal and familial in character. The house, food, horarium, clothing, rhythm of work, Divine Office, hospitality, contact with neighbors, will all be quite different from what has hitherto been done in the great European abbeys and thence imported into Asia. While not sacrificing anything essential but in fact stressing this more clearly, such a development would fulfill the wish of the Council for contemplative houses in mission countries: "By living their life in a manner adapted to the authentically religious conditions of the peoples they will render among them a splendid testimony to the majesty of God, to his love and to the union of Christians."[41]

MONASTICISM AND MISSION

The final question to be faced in any treatment of monasticism in Asia is that of its relationship with the missionary activity of the Church. This may be presented in a variety of ways which we summarize here by two extreme examples showing the full gamut of facts. The first is clear enough, and needs hardly any explanation. Sometimes by force of historical circumstances at the time of their arrival, or by the recent traditions of their country of origin, monks have become heavily involved in apostolic work. This has affected the monastic life itself, and the type of influence properly to be expected of a monastery. This type of thing was certainly normal and beneficial, even inevitable when monasticism was in its initial stages in a Church that was also young, or being renewed; but in proportion to the country's developing beyond the initial stages in education, basic commerce and elementary social

41. *Ad gentes*, no. 40.

justice, there will be a clearer delineation of the personality of each Christian group, each religious institute, and therefore also of monasticism. Monasticism will grow into a fuller awareness of its own identity—of what it is, of what it alone is to become, and consequently of its particular role. By bringing to light its own distinctive characteristics it will become an integrating element in the total activity of the Church—a complement necessary to all other elements. In the meantime, it may profitably run a school or a parish in the way other institutions do, and with hardly any distinctive characteristics. But it must always remain "a school of the Lord's service" as St Benedict wanted, and must become this more and more for the good of the whole Church in each country. It may be said that the necessity for such an evolution is being experienced at present by the young people, who will carry out this program to some extent without prejudice to existing institutions which will have the right to continue.

But there is another very different case; that of the evangelization of aboriginal tribes. These exist in almost every country and are often numerous. It is necessary to recognize that Catholics belonging to races culturally and economically more developed are showing no concern for these people who live beside them and among them. There are historical reasons for this, and they are doubtless admissable. Some of the native clergy admitted quite recently their lack of missionary spirit;" they have the work in this domain to others, such as the Fathers of the Foreign Mission (Paris), who deserve praise in this regard. Let us ask ourselves whether a Christianity is fully a church that maintains itself, defends itself, grows only through its high birth-rate but does not spread, does not have influence, does not announce the message. Fortunately an evolution is in progress on this point too, and something has already begun in monasticism as in other fields. To get away from generalities, I may be allowed to recall some personal memories of one very special case. These are among the finest memories I have from a very long trip. In a Vietnamese monastery I read the book of Fr Dournes, *Dieu aime les paiens*, with a preface by Fr de Lubac.[42] It deals with the Montagnards of the country. Then I read his other work, *Dieu m'a envoyé,*[43] and his article "L'Offrande des peuples," about their liturgy,[44] and finally, *Recueil des coutumes Rhadées du Darlac,* published by L. Sabatier and D. Antomarchi.[45] I had admired the deep faith and moral sense of this people, and their poetic expression—for example, "A big house, as long as the sonorous boom of a gong." A missionary who was working on the study of the religion of the Rhademes had further increased my interest in them. There were a few monasteries that had a Montagnard monk and a few postulants, and I was hoping to have a talk with them.

One day this same missionary took me to visit two villages. These bore hardly any trace of what we call civilization, they had preserved all their ancestral traditions: their religion—they believed in a Supreme Being—their precise moral code, their manner of conduct, clothing, eating, especially their method of constructing villages on a fixed plan and their utilization of timber in building these long houses without the help of any sort of metal. There is a long house for each broad family group its length reminding one of the echoing of a gong. I will pass over the details of hospitality and the visit to the village and to the cemetery which revealed a complete mental and spiritual world. All these people were keenly sensitive to anything of interest. In all their faces one could see a reflection of the mystery of God.

An attempt was being made to begin a monastic community for the women of one of the tribes. A missionary priest had been unable to come, and a nun was charged by the bishop to carry out this plan. One day she took me to the village near which she lived. When people saw that I had come they asked if I would accept their token of Montagnard hospitality. They said it would give them great joy, and that they would take it as a privilege. To accept their hospitality meant drinking rice

42. Paris, 1963. Appearing in English under the title, *God in Vietnam* (London: Geoffrey Chapman, 1965).

43. Paris, 1965.

44. Now appearing in a volume under the same title, Paris: Cerf, 1967.

45. Hanoi, 1940.

beer from a jar. After a walk in the village, we came back to
the house where a meal was being prepared for us. We ate sitting on the floor, which was raised on piles, and there was
rice, pineapples and a dish of banana leaves, as well as all
sort of sauces and spices. When the meal was over, we went
to the large room where visitors were received. A bamboo
mat was brought in and a rice beer ceremony began. A boy
standing near the jar was told to fill it with as much water as
would be needed for drinking; then the head of the family
began to drink, inviting me to do so too. Then it was the nun's
turn. And he called every man and woman living in that house
to come in order of rank and perform this right of friendship.

Then suddenly the head of the house told a boy to direct
the ceremony for him as he wanted to speak to me and tell
me what was in his heart. He asked if I were willing to listen
and then he began. The nun translated. For twenty minutes I
heard the Holy Spirit speaking through the mouth of a simple
man representing a purely spiritual elite that had nothing
cultural or economic to distinguish it—the *electi*, as St Gregory
says, are "those whom God has chosen." What he proceeded
to tell me is exactly what St Gregory has expressed in the
language of the theologian. For this Montagnard is a baptized
Christian, and all in his large family are either baptized or
catechumens. Some of the catechumens have already received
the first rite of adult baptism, or are preparing to do so. I
would have liked to write down every single phrase used by
this witness of God. Everything he said was marked by beauty
and nobility.

He began by telling me that he has a great longing and a
great anguish. He realizes every day that the Montagnards are
poor and weak from every point of view. Humanly speaking
they are undeveloped, but worst of all they are dominated by
Satan who is constantly acting on them and against them by
evil influence and by the wickedness of men. Jesus is the only
one who can lift them out of their spiritual and material
wretchedness. He told me that his one wish is to strive by
every possible means to do something about it—and the nun
translating impressed on me that he used this word "strive"

insistently and several times. He asked me to pray and to get others to pray for these Montagnards and for himself, so that he and his family would always have the courage and strength (again he was emphatic) to serve Jesus, to make him known and to do good among these Montagnards. He said he had no clear light about what God was asking of him. He only knew that he had decided, he had made up his mind, and that he needed help, for he felt that he was alone with Satan and the world. At the end, he expressed a desire to have the Blessed Sacrament reserved in the village: they would build a house and keep guard in prayer; he thought that their only hope was this victorious presence of Jesus among them. I was exceedingly moved, and told him that I would answer him and that the nun would translate. Then for half an hour, I spoke with him of the death and resurrection of Jesus, and of the Spirit of fortitude whom he is sending to us at every instant. I told him about the solitude and the seeming failure of Jesus. He had not been understood, he had been persecuted, rejected, condemned and put to death. But it was this same Jesus who saved us in love and forgiveness. All the young people of the village had gathered round while he was speaking to me, and now they listened to my reply. I added now that just as Jesus had not met with success or gained a great following, neither had he promised them to others. But what counts for us as for Jesus, is our desire, our courageous solidarity, our love which will go so far as to forgive, and our kindness and goodness to all, even to our enemies, Jesus knows and loves each one of these Montagnards personally, I told him, as he knows every member of the whole human race. He wants to save each one. And he does so if they have faith and practice morality according to their tradition, in spite of Satan's influence. For love is the strongest thing of all, and Jesus has gained the victory. He is now in glory, and these few Christian mountaineers can have such knowledge, such courage, faith and charity only because Jesus sends them the Holy Spirit. They must still hope for him, even though he is present. Their life and their efforts have meaning already, are succeeding already, even now they are an influence for good among these mountain people, and in fact, among men. I told them to extend their longings and their prayer and their love to all Vietnamese, and to all men,— whether Christian or not—in Asia, America, Africa, Europe, to the Communists of Russia, China and Vietnam (several of those present were refugees, orphans or victims in one way or another). I told them about the mystery of the whole Church throughout the world, and that it is Jesus present in every place—Jesus to whom he and his family are united in a very real way, by faith and the sacraments, especially the Eucharist, by prayer and by love. As for his wish to keep the Blessed Sacrament in the village, he could tell the Bishop about this, and he would certainly give it careful thought. I told him that I myself thought he would willingly grant this, at least for a short time to begin with. He thanked me and said that he would try and keep all I had said in his heart. Everyone's face was serious, yet smiling and relaxed. Then I embraced each one of the children separately, and met all the adults, both the young men and women and the older folk. I got myself introduced to each one, and asked their name and their age (which several did not know), and also how far each had gone in Christian initiation. It was sheer joy. Then again they offered me to drink from the jar of friendship.

Without doubt, the presence of a missionary with a knowledge of ethnology would have helped me grasp more fully the meaning of this encounter and these rites. But already it was possible to foresee problems whose solution will come when God wills, and in the way he wills.

Here and now, the question we monks and nuns have to face is this: is monastic life nothing but the flower of Christianity? Is it to be allowed to appear only when everything else is already in existence as if monastic life were some sort of luxury line. Some sort of superfluity? It seems from the *Decree on Missionary Activity,* that it is meant to be present in a Church from the very start, and that it is part of putting down firm roots. Quite recently a Montagnard said to me: "Along with men and women for teaching and preaching we need men and women of prayer." He thought that nothing would be accomplished while there was no one to adore the Blessed

Sacrament. The Bishop and others are of the opinion that it is necessary to make a beginning of monastic life among the Montagnards and then wait; to take the risk, and expect from God a reply which might be very slow to come, and perhaps might not come during our lifetime. But a response must be made to this call of the Holy Spirit, to this mission coming from the head of the church. To all who make objections on the grounds of common sense (these folk are never lacking), to all who are obsessed with the idea of rapid success with recruitment and encouraging statistics, the reply may be given that Fr de Foucauld has no disciples until twenty years after his death. Lack of immediate success does not prove that an idea is false or that "prompting" or aspiration does not come from the Holy Spirit.

CONCLUSIONS

All these considerations may seem to be too general, and so they are. They call for definite examples and yet this would not have been prudent; still even as they stand they suffice to show that while the problems are many and serious, they are not insoluble. Let us be wary of those formulas we sometimes hear such as "the tragedy of Asiatic monasticism is . . ." or "Asiatic monasticism got a bad start." The only legitimate attitude is one of patient and realistic optimism.

Realistic in the first place. It is quite true that with a few exceptions almost nothing has been taken or learned from Asia and its cultural, spiritual, religious and monastic traditions—and even where this has been done, there have been clashes, difficulties and misunderstandings. Still, the fact of monasticism remains: it must be helped to achieve its identity and to decolonize itself. We might apply to this situation the words recently spoken by a Chinese theologian: "Christianity must be made indigenous. To this effect indigenous forms of music, architecture, painting and sculpture are welcome expressions of the Christian faith. Moreover, this process of indigenization must go further and deeper. The Christians of Asia must discover the thought-forms in their respective heritages and invest them with new meaning and new depth in the light of the Gospel."[46] All this "after the examples set by the apostles John and Paul, who did not hesitate to 'press into the service of the Gospel the terminology of Greek philosophy, the symbols of mystery religions and the structures of thought of the Gnostics.' "[47]

Dom Winandy years ago pointed out that "Christian monasticism in India must be truly monastic and truly Indian."[48] And Bishop Mendonça, Bishop of Tiruchirapalli, in the preface of a book of Abbé Monchanin and Père le Saulx, has spoken in the same way. "In spite of the growth of the autochthonous clergy, and the creation of dioceses ruled by sons of our own soil, Christianity is always considered here as an imported religion, proof of foreign domination, and a thorn in the foot of the free India."[49] He added: "Once the contemplative life has become truly Indian, Christianization of Indian culture as a whole will follow quite naturally."[50]

The line of conduct for the future was already clear before Vatican II came along to define it still more precisely. In the meantime, Christian monasteries and monks are already in existence. God is being served, loved and praised. Souls are struggling, making present the mystery of the death and resurrection of Christ, praying for the Church and with her. Good is being done, and in multiple ways. Everywhere there is virtue, even holiness itself. All this is of value for eternity, no one could hold that this has never existed. Better still, it is all a preparation, preparing the way for something finer still. We should not hold it cheap. Above all, we should not despair, but work and improve what has been done. Improvement will come mainly through detachment from attitudes previously assumed and through spiritual liberty. It is the concern of each and all, in union with the authorities of the Church. The

---

46. Matthew Chen OP, "Confession de la Foi" in *Concilium* 25 (1967): 157.

47. *Ibid.*

48. Introduction to J. Monchanin and H. le Saulx, *Ermites de Saccidananda* (Paris-Tournai, 1956), p. 11.

49. Preface to the same volume, p. 8.

50. *Ibid.,* p. 9.

witness of the Holy Spirit in many hearts is already responding to this awareness of collective responsibility. Desire is the beginning of eternity, and here below it is the beginning of Christian action.

Realism will be patient as well as confident. Christ accepted time and submitted to it. St Augustine said of Jesus' infancy: "He lay helpless in the crib and he reigned: with patience he waited for his age to increase, he submitted to delay, he by whom time itself was created,"[51] And it is in historic time, "in the day of time" that he became poor by the Incarnation, wrote a Doctor of the African Church.[52] One of the forms of his poverty was his own growth; he grew slowly, secretly over the span of thirty years and for three years of public life. He knew how to wait and in this way taught us to do the same. Results, if not success itself, will follow if the time of waiting in patience has not been lost. And to prepare for it, we must not lose sight of the end which Fr de Lubac and Abbé Monchanin have formulated in regard to India in the following words which are just as valid for the whole church: "Non-Christians are truly entitled to see the Church just as she is in her total mission: turned to men in reflexion and the will to save, but turned primarily towards God in adoration and love."[53]

---

51. *Patienter expectavit aetates, patienter tempora pertulit, per quem facta sunt tempora . . ., Sermon CCXXXIX* 6; PL 38:1129.

52. *Christus in die temporis pauper factus est, ut redimeret nos,* S. Fulgentius de Ruspa, *Sermon II* PL 65:727; the whole context (which is very good) is concerned with the "day of time" in which he lived who is the "Eternal Day."

53. H. de Lubac, *Images de l'abbé Monachanin* (Paris, 1967), pp. 110-111, where we read, "toward men to think (meditate) and to save;" in J. Monachanin, *Eremites du Saccidananda,* p. 22, we find the expression adopted here; both teachings are full of meaning.

MARY THE CONTEMPLATIVE AND
MARY THE APOSTLE[1]

THE SECOND VATICAN COUNCIL has exhorted all religious "to combine an apostolic love with contemplation by which mind and heart are raised to God."[2] This obligation rests upon every Christian whatever his state of life. Now we need to recognize our difficulty in preserving this unity. Almost inevitably there will be some degree of tension, if not actual conflict, between these two elements comprising the one Christian charity. How are we to resolve the problem? We will find help by turning to the one who was the perfect model of both the contemplative and apostolic life as represented in tradition by Mary and Martha. When the feast of the Assumption was introduced into the Western liturgy, the Gospel for the common of virgins was simply taken over for this day. It consisted of the account given in the tenth chapter of St Luke of the episode concerning these two sisters. One of them had simply listened to the Lord whereas the other had done him a service. Monastic commentators on this reading were very fond of showing how the Mother of God, all through her earthly life had perfectly realized and reconciled the two forms of activity represented by these two holy women: the work of prayer and the work of service.[3]

Mary had served the Son of God become her own son.

1. *Miles Immaculatae* 3 (1967): 425-429.
2. *Perfectae Caritatis*, no. 5.
3. In *Études sur le vocabulaire monastique du moyen âge, Studia Anselmiana* 48 (Rome, 1961), pp. 150-151, I have quoted the texts.

Actually, more and better than anyone else, Mary had recognized in her Son the Word of God. She had been full of
careful concern for him and devoted to his person. Writers
love to recall all the services she rendered him from the day
when he was a tiny child. Writers of Northern Europe and
especially of England, a country where hydrotherapy had
always played an important role, have never failed to remind
us that Mary had not only carried her Son in her arms, and
caressed him—they add the delightful detail that she gave him
his bath. She had taken him away to Egypt, and was constantly at his beck and call till that very moment when she
helped to take him down from the cross and bury him. Some
are reminded of this verse of the Song of Songs: "His left hand
is under my head and his right embraces me";[4] the left symbol-
izing the activity of support and help, while the right represents
that of contemplation. In the same way, it was Mary's constant
preoccupation to consider her son, to ponder over him: "She
faithfully kept all these memories in her heart."[5] She had been
living continually in his presence, watching him, listening to
him, loving him. And so, in the most realistic way possible,
she had been the most perfect model of unity between the
two ways of life.

This reminder of the values of the Gospel and Tradition
prepares us to appreciate one of those who has best developed
the theme of the two lives, which find their unity in Mary.
Odo, a twelfth-century monk of Canterbury, in one of his
sermons for the Assumption, has shown that the Mother of
God, who is the Seat of Wisdom, is also the wisdom of Christians, and in this sense, their "philosophy." Here is his text:

> In the Gospel Jesus is described as the guest of two sisters.
> One of them served him and the other just listened to
> what he had to say.[6] This applies to the Blessed Virgin
> Mary.
> These two women customarily represent two ways of life
> in the Church: Martha represents the active life, Mary the

4. Song 2:6.
5. Lk 2:51.
6. Lk 10:38-42.

contemplative life. Martha spent herself in works of mercy; Mary gave herself up to contemplation. The active life is devoted to love of neighbor, whereas the contemplative life is spent in the love of God. Now, Christ is both God and Man. He received the undivided love of the Blessed Virgin Mary for she was devoted to the service of his humanity and to the contemplation of his divinity. A wise man called Mary "the philosophy of Christians," and the first word of this phrase means "love of Wisdom." So just while Christians love to find true wisdom in Mary so was Mary, more than all others, love to serve the humanity and contemplate the divinity of Christ who is the very Wisdom of Christians.

Others serve the members of Christ; Mary served Christ in person, as God's Son and her own. She did this not only by exterior activity, as Martha did, but by her own being; for she gave him the hospitality of her womb. From his earliest childhood she helped the weakness of his human nature, caressing him, giving him his bath, caring for him. When he needed to flee from Herod's persecution, she carried him into Egypt, and then later brought him back. In the end, after all her marvellous service, she stood beside him as he was dying on the Cross, and she was present at his burial. It was then that she suffered, the sharp sword of sorrow piercing her soul, as Simeon had foretold. By all this was she Martha, and who could equal her service?

And in the role of Mary she is again superior to all in her contemplation. In truth, what a contemplative she must have been, who had even borne the divinity within her, united to her flesh, in the person of the Son of God. This Word who from the beginning was with God and was God, is the one whom she bore; then she listened to him, conversed with him, enjoyed him, and contemplated him. "Christ is the Power and the Wisdom of God,"[7] and he was in Mary—so that all the power and wisdom of God were within her. "In Christ are hidden all the treasures of wisdom and knowledge;"[8] and he was in Mary—so that she holds all the treasures of wisdom and of knowledge.

7. 1 Cor 1:24.
8. Col 2:3.

All the plentitude of the divinity is found corporally in Christ, and as he was in Mary, the fullness of the divinity dwelt in her, When the Father dwells in her, the Son and the Spirit dwell in her. Such was the contemplative Mary. Such was she who contemplated the glory of the whole Trinity in God's only Son whom she had begotten in her flesh. Christ shows how the glory of the Trinity is manifested in contemplation when he says: "No one knows the Son but the Father, and no one knows the Father but the Son and he to whom it shall please the Son to reveal him."[9] Now if the Son has sometimes revealed to a mortal being both the Father and himself, in so much as he is Son and the Holy Spirit, how much more clearly would he have revealed himself and the Father and the Holy Spirit to his Mother who, by reason of her purity of heart was to see God more fully than all men. "He who sees me, sees the Father also."[10] No one has seen God as well as his Mother who bore him in her body. "Everything I have learned from my Father," he told his apostles, "I have made known to you."[11] And if he revealed everything to his apostles, would he have hidden something from his mother who is Queen of the Apostles and Confidante of the Trinity? Since Mary has perceived the glory of the Trinity in her Son better than anyone else, her contemplation has certainly been more sublime.

She who is called the "philosophy of Christians" has spent all her life more perfectly than all other men in service of the humanity of Christ and in contemplation of his divinity. We can truly say, then, that only in her has Martha so served and only in her has Mary been so dedicated to contemplation.[12]

In practice, how can we imitate Mary, who is model of the two ways of life. Between Mary's attitude towards Jesus and our own we find there is one element in common; it is faith. And it is Mary's faith upon which the Council has insisted so

9. Mt 11:27.
10. Jn 14:9.
11. Jn 15:15.
12. The Latin text is in *Études sur le vocabulaire*, pp. 152-154.

much, this faith in which she grew and progressed.[13] As in Mary, so also in us, this faith must unite and reconcile the activity of prayer with the activity of service.

Faith in the active life: as mother of God she served her Son in his own person, directly and without intermediary. We do not live with him in the same way; we must serve him in the person of his members. They hold his place among us; we must learn to find him in them. Our eyes do not see him as Mary saw him, and yet, they must shine with the same faith as shone in hers.

Faith in prayer and in the contemplative life: when Mary "kept all these things in her heart" she "did not understand" them all.[14] It is the Gospel itself that gives us these two phrases. Mary's faith remained normal faith, that is, it was obscure, like anyone else's in this state of pilgrimage, in exile in the Church, as the Council reminds us. Our faith is obscure too; but Mary's was so strong that, when almost everyone's faith weakened, between Good Friday and Easter, hers remained absolute and unshaken, as the ancients loved to recall.[15] This faith which enabled Mary to serve and to contemplate her Son so perfectly is the model and beginning of that faith which will bring us to unite the active and the contemplative in our lives also.

13. *Lumen gentium*, ch. 8.
14. Lk 2:50.
15. Texts quoted by Y. Congar, "Incidence ecclésiologique d'un thème de dévotion mariale" in *Mélanges de science religieuse* (1950): 277-292.

CISTERCIAN PUBLICATIONS

Titles Listing

1978